TABLE OF CONTENTS

INTRODUCTION

The terrorist attacks against New York City and Washington D.C. on 11 September 2001, were acts of war against the United States. The U.S. government declared Enduring Freedom and Iraqi Freedom successful and important steps in the war on terrorism. It is, however, premature to declare success in the war on terrorism. Combat operations diminished Al Qaeda's infrastructure and operational capabilities, but Al Qaeda remains a viable international threat. Thus, the challenge to military planners is to develop criteria with which to measure success in the war on terrorism. These criteria should clearly define what military forces must accomplish to set the necessary conditions for success.

Joint planning doctrine requires combatant commanders to define mission success criteria when they issue guidance for the development of military courses of action. These criteria define the measures by which to judge the progress made by military forces toward achieving the desired strategic end-state.[1] Joint doctrine lists the requirement for defining mission success criteria, but provides no insight into a conceptual process for defining the criteria. The conceptual aspect of developing the criteria in a major theater war against a conventional force is not difficult. The difficult task is to develop success criteria against an asymmetric adversary. It is, therefore, necessary to develop a methodology to develop success criteria.

The first step in defining mission success criteria is analysis of the national strategic goals or objectives. The "National Strategy for Combating Terrorism" outlines the strategy to reduce the operational reach and capabilities of transnational terrorist organizations. This document provides the primary direction and guidance for future counter terrorist campaigns and operations. The document outlines strategic success but only in general terms. The strategy does not apply either a qualitative or a quantitative metric to measure success. It is, therefore, the responsibility of military planners to define the operational metrics of success.

The second step in the process involves understanding the operational environment. The step is not in contemporary joint publications, but it is an important in determining criteria in this environment. Planners must understand this type of war. General knowledge about terrorism does not provide a sufficiently detailed basis upon which to form valid success criteria. If military planners proceed from only a general knowledge of insurgency, then the operation will fail before it even begins. The terrorist threat today is transnational in nature. They are well financed, well trained and exploit societal weaknesses. The most relevant aspect of modern terrorist organizations is their global reach. The 911 attacks revealed Al Qaeda's ability to plan, coordinate and execute a complex attack against America. Terrorist operations do not conform to a standard operational procedure or abide by international laws. Al Qaeda is at war with the infidels and violence is justified regardless of the targets and methods employed to achieve their ends. The methods and operations are asymmetric in nature. When parity is not achievable, asymmetric warfare permits the terrorist to attack enemy vulnerabilities and to survive. The asymmetric warfare is alien to the United States' contemporary conventional military training and the Army's mental model. Combating terrorism, therefore, requires a thorough understanding of the environment and the threat. The U S military failed to understand the operational environment during the planning, execution and post-conflict phases of the Operation Iraqi Freedom and did not consider the asymmetric nature of the Fedayeen Sadaam or terrorists operating in Iraq. The military refused to accept the growing threat. The U.S. military's doctrine and training does not address operations in an asymmetric environment.

The third step, which is embedded in the joint planning process, is development of mission success criteria in the war on terrorism based upon the operational environment and the threat. Given the fact that terrorism is not a new phenomenon, history provides insight into developing valid mission success criteria. The U.S. military fought in numerous insurgencies and

---

[1] Joint Publication 5-0 (2nd Draft) *Doctrine for Joint Planning Operations* (10 December 2002),

counterinsurgencies since WWII. In each case, the insurgent forces employed tactics and techniques similar to those of modern terrorist organizations. An analysis of insurgent organizations reveals terrorism as a means to compensate for the lack of parity with the adversaries. It is, therefore, logical to conclude that terrorism is understood by studying insurgencies. Counterinsurgency operations since the end of WWII have revealed a set of principles useful for defining success in counterinsurgencies. These principles are applicable for defining success in combating terrorism.

One student of insurgencies is Dr. Max G. Manwaring. He writes that wars, especially insurgencies, are not simply the sum of battles over time leading to victory. Wars are the product of the elements of national power to achieve the strategic objectives. Each conflict is unique, but they all share common principles. The six principle components of his paradigm are based upon an empirical examination of 43 post-World War II counterinsurgency operations that were either successful or failed. These principles are legitimacy, organization, military support to the targeted government, intelligence, discipline and the capabilities of armed forces and reduction of outside aid to the insurgents. Manwaring's paradigm on insurgency wars provides insight into defining success in counterinsurgencies, but his principles should not be taken on face value alone.

Manwaring's principles combined with an understanding of the operational environment provide the conceptual framework for defining success in the war on terrorism. To this end, the research includes two case studies to assess Manwaring's paradigm. The case studies also revealed the complex nature of the insurgent environment. The first case study was an analysis of the Philippines Huk rebellion, 1946 to 1955. The counterinsurgency operations in the Philippines had two distinct periods that served to reveal common principles. The government's counterinsurgency (COIN) operations from 1946 to 1949 revealed the predictable accuracy of the Manwaring paradigm. By 1949, the Philippine government was near total collapse, and the Huks were preparing to transition to a strategic offensive to overthrow the government. The Philippine government survived due to the efforts of Roman Magsaysay. He was appointed as the Secretary of National Defense and tasked to defeat the insurgency. Magsaysay, a former guerilla fighter, understood insurgencies and how to defeat them. His national campaign to defeat the Huks defined the principles through his actions.

The second case study offered another view of the insurgent environment. The second case study was an analysis of the Armed Revolutionary Front of Colombia (FARC). The FARC case study differs from the previous case study. The Colombian government has waged a decade's long war against the FARC and no end is in sight. The analysis revealed some issues arising from the Manwaring's principles of legitimacy and military support to an effected government. The Colombian government's legitimacy is not the issue. The issue at hand is its ability to establish and maintain control over a substantial area of Colombia. The military support to the Colombian government revealed an issue not addressed in this principle of Manwaring's paradigm. The Colombian government's primary military supporter is the United States. The military support provided by the U.S. has complicated COIN operations. Current U.S. supported operations focus on counter-drug operations as a means to an end, and, consequently, conditions of foreign assistance limit effectiveness of US support Columbia's counter-insurgency.

A NATIONAL STRATEGY TO COMBAT GLOBAL TERRORISM

President Bush's 20 September 2001 address to the nation was the first glimpse into what would later become a national strategy for combating global terrorism. The central theme of that address was the defense of freedom and the defense of peace loving people throughout the world. A key sentence in the speech gave some insight into the strategic objectives of the impending war on terrorism. The objectives were to find, stop and defeat terrorist organizations of global reach.

The strategic objectives are to stop terrorist attacks against America, its interests and allies, and to create an international environment, which denies direct or indirect sanctuary to these organizations. To reach this goal, the strategy outlines five objectives: defeat, deter, defend, diminish and deny.[2] The U.S. and its allies will defeat international terrorist organizations by attacking their sanctuaries: leadership, command and control mechanisms, materiel support, communications networks and financial means. Doing so will disrupt the terrorist organization's ability to plan, coordinate and execute operations against U.S. interests. In conjunction with defeating these organizations, the U.S. will deny sanctuary and sponsorship to terrorists. Achieving this goal is predicated upon the cooperation and participation of foreign governments accepting responsibility as outlined in UNSCR 1373 and the 12 UN counter terrorism protocols and conventions. A difficult objective to achieve is the objective to diminish the underlying conditions, which terrorists seek to exploit. The strategic aim focuses on providing support to countries or regions that are at risk, because these at risk countries are embroiled in internal conflicts.[3]

The strategy defines victory in the war on terrorism as a sustained effort that will reduce the scope and capabilities of terrorist organizations, isolate them regionally, and ensure their destruction within state borders. The strategy, however, does not define the measures of success in the war on terrorism. The objective to diminish, was noted as being the most difficult to achieve. The nations at risk either lack the ability or will to exercise authority and control within their borders in accordance with U.N. resolutions on terrorism. To measure success, planners must look at how these exploitable environments are created and sustained. Planners must then examine what must be done to secure a government at risk. The third requirement is to develop principles by which to measure progress towards defeating an asymmetric threat.

---

[2] Department of Defense. *National Strategy for Combating Terrorism* (Washington , D.C., 2003), 11.

[3] Ibid., 12.

THE OPERATIONAL ENVIRONMENT

Building a knowledge base on insurgencies and terrorism begins with succinct definitions. Joint Publication 1-02 DoD Dictionary of Military and Associated Terms might seem to be the logical place to look to define insurgency, but the definition was too restrictive and did not consider the transnational nature of terrorism and insurgencies. Another source was Bard O'Neil's book on insurgency and terrorism. O'Neil defined insurgency as "a struggle between a non-ruling group and the ruling authorities in which the non-ruling group consciously uses political resources (e.g., organizational expertise, propaganda and demonstrations) and violence to destroy, reformulate or sustain the basis of legitimacy of one or more aspects of politics."[4] Joint Publication 1-02's simple definition of an insurgency, without further research into the subject, leads to a poor understanding of the operational environment.

The current operations in Iraq show the military's doctrinal shortcomings and failure to understand the operational environment. The U.S. military did not understand the operational environment during Operation Iraqi Freedom. Within days of the regime's fall, attacks against American forces began. In the minds of the U.S. government, the war was over, and the priority was the formation of a new Iraqi government. As the number of low-level attacks increased, the press began to question the Pentagon and Secretary of Defense Rumsfeld on the issue. These attacks, in what later became to known as the "Sunni Triangle," were described as the result of "dead enders" and that U.S. and coalition forces would root them out. Rumsfeld further described the enemy as a small number of Iraqis (10-20 personnel), not a large maneuver force or a tightly controlled network. Major General Ray Odierno, 4th ID Commander, described the acts as unorganized, militarily insignificant, having no impact on current operations, purely acts of desperation.[5] The reality was that these "dead enders" were in a strategic defensive, and it was

---

[4] Bard O'Neill, Insurgency and Terrorism: Inside Modern Revolutionary Warfare, (Herndon: Brassey's Inc, 1990), 13.
[5] *Associated Press* (Houston Chronicle), 18 June 2003.

easy to predict that the scope and intensity of the attacks would increase in time. The Philippine and Colombia case studies showed that those two governments and their militaries also failed to understand the nature of the insurgent and terrorist environments.

In the latter half of the twentieth century, the world has faced an increasingly unstable, violent and unpredictable political environment. Since World War II, there has been an average of eight ongoing wars on any given day, and the trend shows no signs of lessening. This trend is not a new phenomenon. Terrorism and insurgency dominated political violence since 1969. From then until now the level of violence and the number of international terrorist acts increased from just fewer than two hundred to over eight hundred per year. Insurgents attempting to achieve political ends conducted the preponderance of these attacks.[6]

The terrorist act of "911" left an indelible mark on the American psyche. Something about that particular attack was significant enough to change the strategic environment. The attack was not the first attack on American soil or against U.S. interests. The first attack against the World Trade Center, the USS Cole and the U.S. Embassies in both Kenya and Tanzania, although significant and well-known acts of terror cannot be compared to"911". The attack on the World Trade Towers crossed a threshold. The threshold was either the number of casualties, impact of the event or both.

At the heart of the new strategic environment is the mind of the insurgent and terrorist. There is a plethora of literature concerning the acts, motivations and methods employed by these groups to achieve their end, but not the terrorist mindset. The intense desire to achieve ideal conditions motivates terrorists. This ideal state is normally political, religious or socially oriented. The mind of the terrorist links the actions required to achieve the ideal state. The terrorist mindset is the product of perceived transgressions and inequities in their society or the external world. In the aftermath of "911", Americans wanted to know why they were hated. The

---

[6] Bard O'Neill, 1.

answer is simple. Al Qaeda believes that American arrogance and imperialism created the current decline in the Arab world. America is therefore the obstacle to the ideal state. It is all too easy to view terrorists as religious fanatics without understanding their point of view. The western mind sees the world through a distorted lens. Western culture does not understand the logic of the terrorist's actions or the perceived grievances, which they choose to solve through violence. Nor do the terrorists understand Western beliefs and views toward terrorist actions and motivations. Terrorists see themselves as deliverers of justice for the slighted. They are also hypersensitive to attacks against their core beliefs and humiliations directed against their cause or actions. They view themselves as the protectors of their ideology, beliefs or society and not as terrorist.

The extreme motivations of terrorists justify their actions and results. Rushworth M. Kidder, a prominent researcher of terrorism, has identified seven key characteristics of terrorists:

1) Oversimplification of issues
2) Frustration about the inability to change society
3) A sense of self righteousness
4) A utopian belief in the world
5) A feeling of social isolation
6) A need to assert his own existence
7) A cold blooded willingness to kill

Given the seven characteristics, terrorism is an absolutist approach to resolving a political problem. Terrorists today have become more ruthless, violent and cunning. This combined with an increasing anti-western bias further compounds the level of complexity in combating terrorism.[7]

The terrorist and insurgent mentality is but one aspect of this complex problem. The other aspect involves the conditions that motivate a person take up arms against an international political body or against its own government. As mentioned earlier, people have taken up arms and rebelled against the ruling political authority in the past. People are not inherently

---

[7] Paul B. Davis, 23

aggressive, but rather have the capacity for violence that manifests itself by course of social conditions. Social conditions alone will not result in political violence. A causal sequence of political violence links social conditions to the actualization of political violence. Ted Robert Gurr's *Why Men Rebel* offers a theory of political violence. The affected populace or a small group, in the case of insurgencies, must develop a level of discontent. Discontent is a function of perceived relative depravation. It is important to define relative deprivation, because it is the underlying cause of social and political violence. Relative deprivation is a perceived discrepancy between a person's value expectations and their value capabilities. Value expectations are the goods and conditions of life to which people believe they are rightly entitled. Value capabilities are the goods and conditions they think they are capable of attaining or maintaining, given the social means available to them. Deprivation motivates people to violence. The intensity level of discontent is proportional to the level of political violence. The politicization of that discontent and the actualization of violent action against political objects and actors are the other two aspects that provide the framework for a theory on political violence.

The model of relative deprivation is tempered by societal variables, which may or may not provide the final catalyst to political violence. Gurr notes societal variables that affect the focus of discontent against a political body or agents are: the cultural and sub-cultural sanctions for overt aggression, the extent and degree of success of past political violence, the articulation and dissemination of symbolic appeals justifying violence, the legitimacy of the political system, and the kinds of responses it makes and has made to relative deprivation.

The current view in the war on terrorism portrays a contemporary movement inspired, motivated and justified by radical religious doctrine. Muslims are not alone in believing in martyrdom or mass murder. Other groups commit acts of murder against pagans, heathens and infidels in the name of God and religion. This mindset will result in future acts of terrorism that are more violent, directed against mass civilian targets and designed to rival the attacks of "911".[8]

In the end, the military must digest the nature of insurgencies and terrorism to develop mission success criteria. For this to happen, a change in the mental model for planning operations is the key to success. Military forces are not combating a distinct military structure based upon either Soviet or U.S. military doctrine. The adversary does not have a standard order of battle or a specific doctrine. Their doctrine is found in their ideology. This ideology, however, refuted by western information operations, is impervious to kinetic or psychological targeting. There is no specific or readily identifiable center of gravity to attack. Their center of gravity is embedded in their ideology, which is linked to their perception of relative deprivation. The mere fact that their perception of relative deprivation is not tied to physical requirements, but ideological requirements. This increases the need to understand fully the adversary rather than refute his beliefs. Students of insurgency often take a very simple approach to determining the center of gravity. They tend to believe that the people are the center of gravity in insurgencies and terrorisms. This is an oversimplification of the complex environment. Despite the operation environment's level of complexity and dynamics, there is a set of principles applicable to defining success criteria in terrorism and insurgencies.

MANWARING PARADIGM

"War is a matter of vital importance to the State; the province of life or death; the road to survival or ruin. It is mandatory that it be thoroughly studied".

Sun Tzu, The Art of War[9]

During the Vietnam, the American leadership failed to understand the nature of the conflict in which they fought. As the war went on, the leadership tried to turn the nature of the

---

[8] Ibid., 22-23.

[9] Samuel B. Griffith, trans, *Sun Tzu: The Art of War* (New York: Oxford University Press, 1963), 63.

war into something that it was not. In the end, the failure to understand the nature of the conflict and the operational environment led to the strategic defeat of the U.S. military in Vietnam. The American response was to kill the enemy, but failed to realize that the war was lost before it even started. The U.S. military did in fact inflict a large number of casualties, yet the enemy continued to fight. Secretary of Defense Robert S. MacNamara concluded that the Vietnamese did not value life. MacNamara's belief was based upon the Pentagon's quantitative metric for defining success in the war. The metric for evaluating success was the "body count". General Vo Nguyen Giap refuted MacNamara's conclusion. Giap stated that the high level of casualties were acceptable because they were fighting a war of liberation and not a conventional war of attrition.[10]

In the aftermath of the Vietnam War and the developing global instability, the military wanted to know what variables were instrumental to winning or losing insurgencies. Then Vice Chief of Staff of the U.S. Army General Maxwell Thurman initiated one such study in 1984. General Thurman wanted a theoretical model based upon the study of 43 post-World War II insurgencies that could predict the success or failure of an insurgency.[11] The U.S. Southern Command's Small Wars Operations Research Directorate's (SWORD) research and analysis resulted in the development of the SWORD model, also known as the Manwaring Paradigm. The paradigm revealed six principles important to the success or failure of insurgencies. These variables are:

1) Legitimacy.
2) Organization.
3) Military and other support to a targeted government.
4) Intelligence.
5) Discipline and capability of the armed forces.

---

[10] Max G. Manwaring, *Internal Wars: Rethinking Problem and Response*, (Carlisle Barracks: Strategic Studies Institute, U.S. Army War College, September 2001). 5.
[11] Ibid., 17.

6) Reduction of outside aid to insurgents. [12]

This paradigm is contrary to the operations conducted in Vietnam, in that it does not view victory in this type of war as simply the sum of the number of tactical battles and enemy losses. It also shows that sheer military power weighted against a smaller force does not guarantee success on the battlefield. [13] In the words of Sun Tzu, "In war, numbers alone confer no advantage. Do not advance relying on sheer military power." [14]

Legitimacy

Manwaring believes that legitimacy is the most important principle in the model. Legitimacy, or lack thereof, is central to an insurgent's ability to undermine the authority of the government and sustain its movement. Governments involved directly or indirectly in counterinsurgencies that fail to understand this dimension will fail. [15] As mentioned previously, the Manwaring paradigm was based upon the analysis of 43 post World War II insurgencies. Historically, those post World War II insurgencies were communist based ideologies: Marxist, Leninist, Maoist and Guevarist. These ideologies developed in the affected countries because the social and political conditions were set for political violence. Communist ideologies offered an alternative government that focused on the rights and needs of the lower social and economic strata. The affected governments' legitimacy was therefore a function of its response to relative deprivation. Perceptions of systemic inequalities or ideological differences are open to exploitation by insurgent forces. Perception management is, therefore, crucial to maintaining legitimacy. Insurgents use propaganda to portray the affected government as illegitimate and incapable of governing. Government actions tend to be repressive in nature, which feeds the

---

[12] Max G. Manwaring, "Toward an Understanding of Insurgency Wars: The Paradigm," in *Uncomfortable Wars: Toward a New Paradigm of Low Intensity Conflict,* ed. Max G. Manwaring, Westview Studies in Regional Security, ed. Wm. J. Olson (Boulder: Westview Press, 1991), 20-24.
[13] Ibid., 20.
[14] Griffith, 122.
[15] Manwaring, 20.

insurgent's propaganda. The cycle of action, reaction and propaganda can lessen a government's moral authority in the struggle. In addition to focusing the paradigm on moral authority, the model should also include the government's response to relative deprivation. The greater the perceived relative deprivation, the greater the propensity for violence. The response to perceived deprivation is a crucial factor in the government's ability to maintain the support of the populace and prevent the insurgents from recruiting or gaining direct or indirect support for their cause. The government's response to relative depravation is measurable and serves as a decisive point along a functional line of operation.

Organization

In conjunction with legitimacy, a government must organize its various institutions and agencies to defeat the insurgency. When confronting an insurgency, a government must organize its agencies to not only respond to insurgent acts, but also structure its military to counter the internal threat. This requires organizations, which may or may not have habitual working relationships, to develop systems to organize, integrate and synchronize information and actions. This organization must also be empowered to implement the necessary changes and take action to secure the affected areas and effectively fight the insurgents. The organization must be developed at the highest level capable of establishing and enforcing policies and developing and refining a national campaign plan to defeat the insurgency and implement reforms.

Military and Other Support to a Targeted Government

Most affected governments need external support to organize structure and train its forces for counterinsurgency operations. The data from Manwaring's study shows that the best method for military support to a targeted government is the "train the trainer" concept. This course of action will maintain the government's current level of legitimacy. The intervention of foreign troops for combat operations is a sign that the government is in crisis and serves as a propaganda tool for the insurgents. Support involves more than tactical combat training. The support must also focus on joint campaign planning, civil military operations and special operations. This support, however, comes with a price in most cases.[16] In the case of U.S. support under foreign internal defense (FID), three conditions must exist: the existing or threatened internal disorder is such that action by the U.S. supports U.S. national strategic goals; the affected nation is capable of effectively using U.S. assistance; and the threatened nation requests U.S. assistance.[17] U.S. military support to counterinsurgencies comes with strings attached. Human rights issues are a cornerstone of American values and shape our commitment to affected governments. Counterinsurgency operations are inherently brutal, so planners must balance the needs of the affected government versus the requirements to support the insurgency.

Intelligence

Intelligence operations are designed to locate, isolate and assist in the destruction of insurgent bases and personnel. If an intelligence apparatus is not in place or is ineffective, the insurgents are free to operate in the environment and exploit government weaknesses. Manwaring combines intelligence and psychological instruments into the same principle. The two are separate mechanisms for countering an insurgency and should be separate principles. Information operations in a counterinsurgency serve the purpose of refuting insurgent propaganda and shaping the behavior of the populace. If the effected government does not have an information apparatus that can target the segment of the population at risk, the ruling government may lose those people to the insurgents.

---

[16] Manwaring, 20-23.
[17] Joint Publication 3-07.1. Joint Tactics, Techniques and Procedures for Foreign Internal Defense, (26 June 1996), viii.

Discipline and Capability of the Armed Forces

Manwaring believes that the affected government must have a highly trained, professional and equipped security force capable of rapid decisive operations to achieve the strategic objectives. Discipline plays a critical role in this effort. Insurgents and terrorists do not adhere to the rules of law, and conduct operations as they see fit. Insurgents temper their actions to a certain degree because of the impact their actions may have on their support base. Insurgents use terrorism as a tactic to prevent the populace from openly affecting their operations or to ensure support for their cause. Terrorists, on the other hand, purposely target the adversary's civilian populace. Military operations tend to be the most visible aspect of COIN operations. The military is a functioning arm of the government, and its level of discipline is a reflection of the government. Insurgent and terrorist operations frustrate military efforts, because the adversary can choose the time and place of the attack, and avoid decisive battle with a professional military. This frustration often leads to oppressive military actions directed at the civilian populace. In order to reduce support to the insurgents, military forces employ population resource control measures. These measures segregate the population and materiel resources from the insurgents. In doing so, militaries have historically used oppressive measures to achieve this segregation. This further erodes the legitimacy of the government and may increase support for the insurgents.

Military capability is the second aspect of the military support principle. The adversary is highly capable, and adaptive. The military, therefore, must develop the capability to counter this method of war. Developing a capable force is not a simple task. Conventional forces have historically under performed when combating insurgencies. It is, therefore, necessary to develop an unconventional capability to counter the insurgents. The capability should focus on small unit reconnaissance, raids, strikes and operations in an austere environment. The unconventional approach also requires a greater degree of trust between the leadership and its subordinates.

Reduction of Outside Aid to the Insurgents

This dimension requires internal and external political, military and economic support to separate the insurgents from their base of outside support. This external support includes, arming and equipping, providing sanctuary, positive politicization of the insurgency, funding and combatants.[18] The analysis of insurgencies shows that there are two types of external support: direct and indirect. Direct support involves actively and knowingly providing material support to sustain the insurgents. Indirect support involves using civilian support without their knowledge. Reducing outside aid to the insurgents requires synergy and balance. The task is to separate the insurgents both physically and temporally. This principle supports the final destruction of insurgent organization. It is, therefore, necessary for the effected government to isolate the insurgent from the populace and second country governments defeat the movement.

THE HUKBALAHAP IN THE PHILIPPINES

Background

The Philippine insurgency case study assessed the applicability of the Manwaring paradigm. The Philippine case study was an analysis of the Huk insurgency from 1946 to 1951. The case revealed principles similar to Manwaring's paradigm and the complexities of the operational environment. The Huk insurgency had two distinct periods. During the first phase of the counterinsurgency campaign, the Philippine government treated the problem as a law enforcement issue and not as a threat to national security and survival. The government failed to appreciate the threat, which resulted in its near collapse. The Philippine Constabulary (PC), known as the Military Police Command (MPC) was assigned the mission of destroying the Huks. There is no evidence to suggest that this campaign included actions and legislation to address the

---

[18] Manwaring, 23-24.

social, political and agrarian issues that were at the center of the Huks' strategic aim.[19] In the second phase, the Secretary of National Defense, Ramon Magsaysay, implemented measures that changed the course of the insurgency. He developed and implemented a counterinsurgency campaign plan that led to the defeat of the Huks.[20] Through his actions and understanding the operational environment, he defined the Manwaring principles.

Phase One: A Government in Crisis

The Nacionalista Party, under the leadership of Manuel Quezon and Sergio Osmena won the first Philippine Assembly elections in October 1907. The Nacionalista Party was very effective governing at the local levels, but was more concerned with personal interests and local policy than national governance. That turned out to be the Party's greatest mistake. The party, which dominated Philippine politics until World War II, failed to address issues of land reform, social reform, tenancy rights, population growth and the distribution of wealth. Philippine democracy failed to solve the issues of the Spanish legacy.

The roots of communism and socialism in the Philippines date back to the Comitern expansion of the 1920s.[21] The Comitern's intent was to establish secured footholds in English colonies in Asia. The ideology's nationalistic appeal combined with the effects of economic deprivation in the Asian colonies made its spread possible.[22]

The introduction and growth of the Socialist Party of the Philippines, in 1929, was largely due to the efforts of Pedro Abad Santos. His primary objective was to ensure that poor farmers benefited from the agrarian wealth.[23] The mechanism to spread this was the newly formed

---

[19] A.H.Peterson, G.C. Reinhard and E.E. Conger, eds., Symposium on the Role of Airpower in Counterinsurgency and Unconventional Warfare: The Philippine Huk Campaign, (Santa Monica: RAND, RM-3652-PR, July 1963), 9
[20] Lachica, 21.
[21] Eduardo Lachica, *The Huks: Philippine Agrarian Society in Revolt*, (New York, Praeger Publishers, 1971), 82.
[22] Ibid., 90.
[23] Ibid., 82.

Partido Kommunista ng Philipinas (PKP, Philippine Communist Party) in 1930. The PKP's

political role in the 1930s was small because the Philippine government considered the party a

subversive group, and many of its members were either imprisoned or exiled. Instead of drawing

support from the peasantry, the PKP drew its support laborers. Evangalista, a ranking PKP

leader, believed that the urban proletariat would serve as the mass for a revolutionary movement

in the Philippines. [24]

In 1929, Jacinto Manahan, a former prominent member of the PKP, broke ties with the

communist party and formed the *Kalipunang Pambansa ng mga Magbubukid sa Philipinas*

(KMPK). Manahan left the PKP because he felt that it did not advance the peasant's cause.[25]

Luis Taruc organized the *Aguman ding Maldang Talapaobra* (AMT) in 1932, and later became

the Secretary General of the Socialists Party.[26]

Before the Japanese invasion of the Philippines, several small groups formed together to

oppose Japanese fascism. The three most prominent groups were the League for the Defense of

Democracy, the Communist Party (PKP) and the Friends of China. These groups were clearly

anti-Japanese, and they organized boycotts of Japanese stores and goods. The boycott's intent

was to slow down the Japanese occupation of countries. The three groups also held fundraisers to

collect money, food and clothing for China.[27]

After the Japanese invasion in 1941, representatives from the League for the Defense of

Democracy, the PKP and the Friends of China met in Manila to discuss further actions. The

meetings ended with two key decisions concerning the defense of the Philippines. The first was

that the groups would set aside their ideological and political differences in order to establish a

united front against Japan. The second decision authorized the top leadership of the PKP, Pedro

---

[24] Benedict J. Kerkvliet, *The Huk Rebellion: A Study of Peasant Revolt in the Philippines,* (Berkley: University of California Press, 1977), 50.
[25] Lachica., 100.
[26] Ibid., 89.
[27] Kerkvliet., 96.

Abad Santos and Crisanto Evangelista, to announce their "national unity for an Anti Japanese Front". The two were also authorized to recommend to President Manuel Quezon and American High Commissioner Francis B. Sayre that they begin to organize and train civilians to fight against the Japanese. The representatives reasoned that both Evangelista and Santos should make the recommendation because the government would not expect the PKP to support the war effort. If the PKP were giving its support, the laborers and peasants would follow suit. In short, the PKP pledged its allegiance to the Philippine and United States governments.[28]

Quezon and Sayre refused their offer of support in the defense of the Philippines. The two feared that a national led communist resistance to the invasion would lead to a communist takeover after the war. Their fears were not groundless. The AMT and PKP supporters were urged to form communist governments in areas liberated from Japanese occupation. This order implied a strong and centralized underground movement without hinting that the Communists were best suited and capable to lead the entire resistance effort.[29] Despite the government's refusal to accept assistance, the PKP urged all "anti-fascists" organizations, including the AMT and KPMP, and labor unions to prepare for a massive guerilla war against the impending Japanese invasion.[30] The PKP assumed command and control of the KPMP and AMT after the invasion.[31]

The Japanese invasion of the Philippines in December 1941 enabled a small number of untrained and disorganized communist rebels to become an effective fighting force because it allowed them to expand their base of support. The Japanese occupation of the Philippines allowed the PKP to further its cause under the cover of "patriotic freedom fighters" against a numerically superior force. Evangelista knew that he did not have the mass and unity at the time of the invasion to fight the Japanese, so he took to the Luzon Mountains with a small band of

---

[28] Ibid., 97.
[29] Lachica., 103.
[30] Lachica., 103.

activists. He established his base of operations in Mount Arayat, which provided his small force space and time to form a unified force and to plan for operations against the invaders. [32]

On 10 December 1941, Evangelista issued a manifesto that declared the PKP's support of the Commonwealth of the Philippines and the United States in their defense of the Philippines. Given the resistance force's weakness, Evangelista directed limited ambushes and raids against the Japanese-controlled Philippine Constabulary Police, whose mission was to suppress opposition in the countryside. Evangelista's limited attacks served four important purposes. First, it allowed the PKP to acquire arms and ammunition, which were always in short supply. Second, it convinced many of the constabulary to join the resistance effort to avoid execution. Third, the operations showed the peasants that there was an organized resistance movement, which prevented many of the villages from accepting total Japanese domination. Finally, the limited offensive operations intimidated the constabulary, because the resistance forces could strike at any time and fade back into the countryside. [33]

On 29 March 1942, the PKP merged with the remaining socialists and peasant organizations and formed *Hukbo ng Bayan Laban sa Hapon* (Hukbalahop or Anti-Japanese Army). The newly formed resistance organization selected a four-person military committee. The committee had two missions: waging the guerilla campaign against the Japanese, and seizing power after the war. Luis Taruc was selected as the first Huk commander or "El Supremo". [34]

The basis of the Huk fighting forces was the squadrons. These squadrons consisted of 100 men, led by a commander, an executive officer and an intelligence officer. These squadrons were further broken down into platoons and squads. Two squadrons formed a battalion, and two or more battalions formed a regiment. Each regiment was operationally responsible for one of the five geographically based military districts. The Military Committee in conjunction with the PKP

---

[31] Greenberg p13.
[32] Lawrence M. Greenberg p 13.
[33] Ibid., 14.

formed the Huk General Headquarters (GHQ). Luis Taruc served as the chairman and Casto Alejandrino served as the vice chairman. Political officers were placed at all levels of command to advise the commanders on matters pertaining to civil affairs and indoctrination.[35]

In addition to their military and political capabilities, the Huk clearly understood that they needed auxiliary support to remain a viable force. The Japanese were indirectly responsible for providing the auxiliary support base. The Japanese established neighborhood organizations within occupied villages to facilitate communication with the occupying forces. People with the Huk resistance secretly converted these associations into Barrio United Defense Corps (BUDC). This allowed villagers to appear as if they were obeying the demands of the Japanese government, while in reality, they were procuring and distributing supplies, money and information to the guerillas[36]

The Huk recruitment objectives progressed more slowly than desired, primarily due to the efforts of the United States Army Forces Far East (USAFFE) guerilla units. The U.S. successfully recruited the majority of support because their presence was well known on the islands, as well as, their superior training and organized logistical system. Despite recruitment problems, the Huks still emerged after the war with a 15,000 man, well armed, and well trained force, fully capable of overthrowing the Philippine government.[37]

By February 1945, Manila had been liberated, and the Huks had killed approximately 25,000 Japanese and Filipino collaborators and had fought in over 1,200 combat missions. Their strength had swelled to at least 5,000 men, 10,000 lightly armed reserves and about 25,000 unarmed reserves.[38] The unresolved issue was the air of suspicion that the U.S. held towards the

---

[34] Ibid., 15.
[35] Greenberg., 20.
[36] Kerkvliet., 94.
[37] Greenberg., 16.
[38] Kenneth M. Hammer, "Huks in the Philippines," *Military Review*, (April 1956), in *Modern Guerilla Warfare: Fighting Communist Guerilla Movements, 1941-1961*, ed. Franklin M. Osanka, (New York: Free Press, 1967), 179.

Huk. An October 1944 report released by General MacArthur's headquarters, GHQ Southwest

Pacific Area (SWPA) portrayed the Huks as thieves and murders, who were willing to take up

arms against USAFFE forces. The US perception of the Huks shaped U.S. policy in the

Philippines from 1945 forward.[39] The U.S. showed no interest in recognizing the Huk's

contribution to the war, nor did they receive rewards for their efforts. The US Army exacerbated

the Huk resentment by is continued hostility toward Huk fighters due to their Marxist beliefs.[40]

The final blow to the Huks came with the arrest and seven-month imprisonment of Taruc and

Alejandrino by the U.S. Army Counter Intelligence Corps. The men were arrested on charges of

sedition and murder, but were later released when no evidence supported the charges. Taruc and

Alejandrino took advantage of their arrests and lack of back pay. They immediately reclaimed

command of the Huks and continued with their movement. The Huk political and economic

movement then focused on landlords, the constabulary and the Philippine Army. Their goals

were the elimination of any collaborators from positions of power, a broadening of democracy in

the Philippines through greater worker representation and independence from the U.S.[41]

The Huks and the PKP transformed into the Democratic Alliance (DA) in June 1945.

The DA was designed to legitimize their communist aspirations in the post-war Philippines by

participating as a legal and sanctioned political organization.[42] On the agrarian front, Mateo del

Castillo and Juan Feleo combined the KPMP and the AMT to form the *Pambansang Kaiasahan*

ng mga Magbubukid (National Peasants Union, PKM).[43] Luis Taruc, foreseeing Philippine

independence in accordance with the Tydings-McDuffie Act, knew that he could use the DA to

---

[39] Greenberg., 27.
[40] Hammer., 179.
[41] Ibid., 180.
[42] Greengerg., 28.
[43] Lachica., 119.

establish a base of power within the political system. This in turn would enable achievement of his final objective, seizing control of the Philippine government.[44]

The DA scored an impressive victory in the 23 April 1946 elections. All DA candidates in Central Luzon won congressional seats; two of which went to Taruc and Alejandrino. The DA's success, however, was short lived. Accusations of election fraud ran rampant due to reports of pre-election violence in the districts won by the DA. These accusations caused a Liberal controlled Congress to approve legislation nullifying the elections. The DA presented their case before the Supreme Court, but the legislation upheld the election results, and the DA congressional seats were lost.[45]

The ejection of the DA from Congress created heated tensions in Central Luzon. President Roxas (elected 23 April 1946) attempted to placate the peasants by allowing them to commission their own representative. Roxas' attempts, however, were short lived. On 24 August 1946, uniformed personnel apprehended and executed Juan Feleo and other DA representatives. The assassination of the representatives and the ejection from Congress were the final provocations for the Huks. An insurgency was now the only means by which to achieve the objectives of the DA.[46]

At the beginning of the insurgency, the Huks were composed of three types of people: political (communists and socialists), former wartime guerilla fighters, and a small criminal element. Luis Taruc would have preferred to separate the movement from the criminal element, but the current situation required him to select recruits from anywhere. This reliance on selecting and retaining the diversity among the Huks proved to be detrimental in the 1950s when the government executed an effective counterinsurgency campaign.[47]

---

[44] Greenberg., 28.
[45] Lachica., 121.
[46] Ibid., 121.
[47] Greenberg., 47.

In response to the Huks taking up arms and declaring war on the Philippine government, President Roxas swore to put an end to the insurrection within sixty days. Roxas made the declaration without an appreciation of the Central Luzon situation and the capabilities of his military force. The Military Police had been demobilized and were undermanned. It was also not trained to conduct operations against the Huks' unconventional fighting tactics.[48] The MPC was not organized to conduct COIN operations in support of the government. In the post WW II Philippines, the MPC primary task was law enforcement. The government selected the MPC for this task because they saw the Huks as a criminal organization and not an insurgent group. The Manwaring paradigm principle of organization was not present during this phase oft the COIN operation. The MPC's lack of training, capabilities and brutality resulted in the deaths of numerous innocent civilians, which only fanned the anti-government sentiment.

President Roxas attempted to alleviate the situation by implementing land reform legislation to appease the Huks. The Agrarian Commission implemented a crop-sharing law that returned 70 percent of the harvest to the peasants. This legal gesture did not appease the Huks at all, because their aim was the overthrow of the government.[49] In February 1947, Luis Taruc outlined Huk "minimum terms of peace":

1) The immediate enforcement of the bill of rights, especially the right to assemble, freedom from arbitrary arrests, ending of cruel and unjust punishment, trial by unprejudiced judges.
2) Dismissal of all charges against Huks, MPs, and civilian guards. Release all political prisoners.
3) Replacement of fascists-minded officials in municipal and provincial governments and the Municipal Police Command in the provinces affected by the agrarian unrests.
4) Restoration of all Democratic Alliance congressmen to their seats
5) Implementation of President Roxas' land reform program beginning with a foolproof 70-30 crop distribution law and leading toward eventual abolition of tenancy.[50]

---

[48] Lachica, 21
[49] Ibid., 121.
[50] Kerkvliet, 171.

The Huk's surrender conditions included general amnesty, disbandment of the armed forces, and re-seating the DA in Congress. These impossible demands left Roxas no other course but the "mailed fist" approach to ending the insurgency.

In May 1947, Roxas declared open season on the Huk insurgents. The Philippine Military Police Command, reorganized after the war with the Police Constabulary, joined Civil Guards to hunt the Huks wherever they hid. This gloves off approach to fighting the Huks without regard for rules of law, led to disaster. These government-sanctioned troops pursued the Huks and spread terror throughout the countryside. They were responsible for stealing food and other needed supplies, but most notably, they indiscriminately tortured or intimidated Filipinos. The use of indiscriminate force against the guerillas and the populace created a situation in which the people were more inclined to support the Huks. The unintended consequence of these actions was increased direct and indirect popular support for the Huks.[51] The increased popular support for the Huks was the first sign the government was losing legitimacy and moral authority.

In response to these actions, the Huks returned to their protective guerilla environment deep in the Mount Arayat (Huklandia) region. Just as this environment protected the insurgency from the Spanish, Americans, and Japanese, it would once again protect them from the Philippine government. During this strategic defensive, the Huks managed to create an effective intelligence network that permeated Philippine government agencies and the population. The intelligence network coupled with an ineffective adversary, and their PSYOP program further fueled the Huks' success.[52] The period of hit and run tactics went from 1946-1948. The government's attempt to counter the guerillas through numerous offensive operations was ineffective against this unconventional threat. The key facet of this failure was their inability to produce affects in the Central Luzon region (Huklandia).[53]

---

[51] Greenberg, 45.
[52] Ibid., 49-52.
[53] Kerkvliet, 174-178.

A turning point in the political turmoil came when President Roxas died in April 1948. His vice president Elpidio Quirino replaced him. Quirino attempted accommodation in lieu of confrontation to end the insurgency. Despite Taruc's dictatorial demands, Roxas agreed in principle for the sake of agrarian peace to end the fighting until a permanent settlement could be reached. Taruc regained his position in the Philippine congress and collected two years of his salary and allowances.

The period of peace lasted only two months. Taruc accused the government of negotiating in bad faith and not seriously addressing agrarian needs. In response, he returned to the hills and vowed that the Huks would not surrender until the agrarian issues were settled. The Huks also renamed themselves as the *Hukbong Magpapalaya ng Bayan* (HMB: People's Liberation Army).[54]

Taruc knew that the agrarian issues would not be settled as long as Quirino was the president. He found a political partner in Senator Jose P. Laurel. Laurel was the former wartime president and was the Nacionalista candidate for the presidency in the November 1949 elections. The HMB, despite its anti-collaboration beliefs, were willing to ally with the Nacionalistas to ensure the overthrow of Quirino[55]. President Quirino was re-elected in what became known as the bloodiest and most scandalous election in Philippine history. The attempt to maintain Quirino in power through fraud further exacerbated the problems. The Filipinos lost faith in the election process and the promise of land reform. The 1949 election debacle is important because it was the government's chance to regain some level of legitimacy. Manwaring states that legitimacy was a crucial principle in the paradigm, and the Philippine government lost its moral authority because of the elections. The 1949 elections marked a pivotal point in the insurgency. The Huks now had the moral authority for action. The government was morally corrupt, and the Huks represented a viable alternative. The election results also provided the Huks with a powerful

---

[54] Lachica, 122.

propaganda message. The HMB used these grievances to their advantage and integrated the issues into PSYOP themes to gain additional support for their cause. The HMB also stepped up their attacks against government forces and institutions while the government's control and legitimacy eroded to near failure.[56] The conditions presented a situation favorable to overthrow. Insurgents need tangible factors to show that the current situation is far from their perception of an ideal condition. The Philippine government gave the Huks the needed tangible factors to support their ideal condition, which was a communist based government. The 1949 elections and governmental terrorism provided tangible factors.

Another sign of the Philippine government's near collapse was the ongoing financial crisis caused by corruption and nepotism. This condition further supported the HMB cause and reinforced the belief that the government was incapable of fulfilling its constitutional duties. Additionally, corruption in government and a state of near governmental collapse bolstered the communists' call to immediate action in light of the "revolutionary situation". In January 1950, Jose Lava, CPP leader, called for the overthrow of the Philippine government, and advanced the timetable for the overthrow by nearly two years.[57] This change in the timeline called for a "geometric expansion" of the HMB from 10,000 to 172,000 fighters by September 1951 and for the establishment of "provisional revolutionary governments" in liberated towns and barrios. The party also planned for the transformation of the HMB from a guerilla force to a regular army force when the time was right.[58]

The Philippine government placed its moral authority and legitimacy in jeopardy at the very outset of the Huk rebellion. President Roxas immediately declared the Huks a criminal organization and tasked the MPC with the mission of destroying them. This course of action did

---

[55] Ibid., 123.

[56] A.H. Peterson, G.C. Reinhard and E.E. Conger, eds., Symposium on the Role of Airpower in Counterinsurgency and Unconventional Warfare: The Philippine Huk Campaign, (Santa Monica: RAND, RM-3652-PR, July 1963), 15.

[57] Greenberg, 63.

not address the underlying social and economic conditions, the primary cause of the insurgency. In its endeavor to destroy the Huks, the government committed acts of terror against the population, which it was sworn to protect.

The government further undermined its legitimacy by manipulating the 1949 elections. These elections, called the bloodiest in Philippine history, further alienated the populace. Events supported the HMB's propaganda messages and created a greater base of support. In conjunction with this problem, the government suffered from corruption, nepotism and was in the middle of a financial crisis. The financial crisis meant that the government did not have the means to address any social issues to end the insurgency even if it chose to do so. The more relevant consequence of the financial issue was the government's inability to pay its military forces and equip them. If the government failed to pay the military, it would lose the military's support. This would seal the government's fate.

Phase Two: Defeating the Huks

On 29 March 1950, the HMB launched simultaneous attacks in two towns and 15 barrios. The HMB immediately seized the San Pablo City and destroyed a PC outpost. The second wave of attacks occurred on 26 August. The guerillas successfully overran Camp Macabulos and looted the military bases stocks. While the HMB was reveling in their success, the government was quickly formulating plans to counter and defeat the insurgency.

The Philippine government finally admitted, given the new insurgent offensive, that the PC was incapable of defeating the insurgency. Quirino transferred 3,000 PC troops back to the regular army, placed the PC under the army's operational control and transferred the counterinsurgency responsibilities from the Department of the Interior to the Department of National Defense. By far, Quirino's most ambitious move was to accept the resignation of the

---

[58] Lachica, 127.

defense secretary, and to appoint Ramon Magsaysay to the position.[59] Magsaysay was also an excellent choice because the critical Philippine press viewed him as incorruptible.[60]

The new defense secretary had a background as a guerilla fighter, but lacked formal military training.[61] Before WWII, Magsaysay worked as a bus company manager in Manila. At the outbreak of hostilities, he quit his job and joined the Philippine 31st Division. After the fall of Bataan, he joined a USAFFE guerilla unit as a captain. He distinguished himself throughout the war and later commanded the Zambales Military District with nearly 10,000 guerilla fighters under his command. Magsaysay was elected to the House of Representatives and served on the House Committee on National Defense after the world. It was in this capacity where he fought for veteran's rights and compensation for war service.

In 1950, while Magsaysay was the Chairman of the Armed Services Committee, he traveled to the U.S. to obtain financial assistance for his beleaguered government. His trip was important for two reasons. First, he received $10 million from the Truman Administration, which allowed the Philippine government to pay its troops and solicit information for cash. Second, he met and befriended LTC Edward G. Lansdale. Lansdale was an U.S. Air Force intelligence officer, and had operational experience in the Philippines. This friendship was important because Lansdale was to become Magsaysay's personal Joint U.S. Military Advisory Group (JUSMAG) advisor. Magsaysay understood the important role that the U.S. could play in ending the Huk insurgency. At this point, the government lacked the financial means to pay its soldiers and reorganize the force to counter the insurgency. The military support to the Philippine government included materiel, training and advisors. Upon his return to the Philippines, Magsaysay reported to Quirino that the American government had a low opinion of the Philippine government

---

[59] Ibid., 130.
[60] Hammer, 181.
[61] Lachica, 130.

because of the corruption within the government and the deteriorating social conditions. Quirino ignored the report and told Magsaysay to restrict his attention to military matters.

The deteriorating situation and pressure from MG Leland Hobbs, Chief JUSMAG, prompted Quirino to approach Magsaysay and offer him the position as Secretary of National Defense. Magsaysay agreed to accept the position if he were given a "free hand" in fighting the HMB.[62] Magsaysay first went to work at reorganizing the military and its leadership, and regaining the military's legitimacy.

Magsaysay first relieved the Chief of the PC and the Chief of Staff of the Army. Other high ranking officers who were reluctant to take field assignments were relieved as well.[63] These officers contributed to the problem, because they failed to enforce discipline within the military as evidenced by the level of corruption and acts of terrorism against the populace. Their acts directly contributed to Philippine government's loss of legitimacy. He saw the military as the primary institution that could defeat the Huks and restore the government's legitimacy. He then visited army units and promoted aggressive leaders to command positions. He also relocated some BCTs to different areas within the Philippines to break up suspected corrupt relations that formed between the military and the local populace. These visits were also intended to assess the morale, leadership, equipment and training of army units. To raise the morale of the troops, he used the funds from the U.S. to raise the salary of enlisted troops by threefold. The increase in pay to one peso a day may not seem significant, but it gave soldiers the necessary funds to pay for their daily rations instead of stealing from the peasants.[64]

In a further effort to regain the trust of the populace, he instituted a free direct telegraph service in the villages. This service allowed villagers to send complaints of military misconduct directly to the government and was a step towards restoring discipline within the military. Within

---

[62] Greenberg, 80-81.
[63] Ibid.,, 83.
[64] Ibid., 85.

a matter of months, the outlook and discipline of the AFP improved to an acceptable level.[65] The next challenge for Magsaysay was to improve the capability of the AFP.

The AFP needed relief from the ongoing combat operations to implement organization changes. The break came by way of pure luck. Tarciano Rizal, a Huk informant, fell into Magsaysay's hands. Rizal was willing to cooperate with the government and offered information, which would reveal the location of the CPP Politburo in Manila. On 18 October, Rizal's tip led to the arrests of the communist members. The arrests not only demoralized the movement, but also separated Manila from the Huks, thereby leaving the insurgents half-blind and isolated in the mountain region.[66] The arrests also prompted Magsaysay to get Quirino to issue a proclamation suspending the writ of habeas corpus for the duration of the campaign. That step allowed the government to hold captured guerillas for longer than twenty-four hours without prima facie evidence. By doing so, it not only allowed the AFB to build a case for convicting guerillas, but also prevented them from returning to their guerilla units.[67]

To fight the HMB militarily, Magsaysay advocated a change in tactics and operations. He was still favored large offensive operations, but this problem required a focus on small unit tactics to achieve the desired affects. The Huks had the initiative because they were able to defeat an untrained and undisciplined MPC. The MPC was woefully unprepared and untrained to execute Roxas' "mailed fist" course of action. As with many untrained forces conducting COIN, the Huks, demoralized and defeated the MPC in every engagement. This disparity in capability caused fear and frustration within the armed forces. The fear was so pervasive that soldiers would not venture from the roads or conduct night operations. In their frustration, the military turned to terrorizing the populace as a method to deny support to the Huks. The military was guilty of robbery, rape, murder, bribery, and other crimes committed against the populace.

---

[65] Ibid., 86.
[66] Lachica, 131.
[67] Greenberg, 129.

Magsaysay knew that the military was important to restoring a security to the Philippines. He developed a two-pronged approach defeat the Huks, and to regain the confidence and trust of the people. Magsaysay conducted campaign planning at the national level to ensure synergy and synchronization of the efforts and monitoring.

Magsaysay placed the training focus on squad and platoon night patrolling and hit and run tactics. He believed that these tactics would place continuous pressure on the insurgents and focus intelligence efforts. In his speech to the Philippine General Staff, he educated his officers on the unorthodox methods of insurgents and how the AFP must adapt the military to defeat this threat.[68] Magsaysay bolstered these new tactics by building the AFP to meet the mission requirements. The force increased to 26 BCTs with four tactical level commands. With assistance from JUSMAG and financial aid from the Military Defense Assistance Program (MDAP), the force increased by 28,000 troops by 1955. The AFP required not only military capabilities, but also civic-mindedness. He knew that the terror tactics employed by the PC had to end immediately. From his days as a guerilla leader, he understood that the trust and allegiance of the population was vital to the guerilla campaign. Government attempts to aid the population could be destroyed in a single unjust act. He, therefore, assigned the military dual roles: ambassadors to the people and soldiers against the Huks. He also allowed peasants to utilize military counsel, free of charge, when disputes between landlords and tenants arose. The measure of success was evident months later, when children would run towards soldiers as they entered villages rather than away to hide.[69]

In addition to the combat aspects of the campaign plan, Magsaysay implemented economic measures and incentives further separating the populace from the guerillas and boosting the government's legitimacy. The first was the weapons buy-back program. Under that program, the government recovered over 15,000 weapons, 110,000 hand grenades and over 14 million

---

[68] Greenberg, 87.

rounds of ammunition within a four-year period. The second economic program was the

Economic Development Corps Project (EDCOR).[70] EDCOR provided an alternative to

involvement in the insurgency. Former guerillas received a plot of farmland, outside of the

Luzon region, and provided the basic necessities to get their farms established. As part of the

civic action program, the military controlled the project, and soldiers assisted in all aspects of

helping resettled people.[71] The program was wildly successful and provided Magsaysay with an

additional propaganda victory. He, and not the insurgents, was providing "land for the

landless".[72]

In response to the October 1950 raid and arrest of the CPP Politburo, the HMB launched

a series of raids, kidnappings and acts or terrorism. One notable raid by a Huk squadron in

November 1951 indirectly supported the government's efforts to win over the population. A Huk

squadron attacked and nearly massacred the entire village of Aglao despite the fact that the

villagers had done nothing to anger the Huks. Word of the atrocity quickly spread throughout the

region shocking the population. In an attempt to mitigate the psychological impact, Taruc tried

and convicted the squadron commander, but the damage was done. The Huks never recovered

from this incident.[73]

With the massacre at Aglao and other Huk raids, the AFP launched a new offensive.

With information gathered in the October Manila raid, the AFP launched OPERATION SABER.

The operations purpose was to show the Huks that the government was resolved to take the fight

to insurgent strongholds, and that the government was taking the initiative by launching attacks

when and wherever it chose. In conjunction with this operation, the military began severing lines

of communication between villages and jungle safe havens. With information gained from

[69] Ibid., 88.
[70] Dana R. Dillon, "Comparative Counter-insurgency Strategies in the Philippines," *Small Wars and Insurgencies* 6, no. 3, (Winter 1995), 290.
[71] Ibid., 89.
[72] Greenberg, 91.

infiltrations, informants and aerial reconnaissance, the military intended to separate the guerillas from their popular bases of support. The military also targeted farms, which produced crops for the Huks. These actions further isolated the guerillas, forced the Huks to protect their farms, and put them under continuous pressure. Targeting Huk farms effectively seized the initiative from the Huks. It is important to note, that these operations in conjunction with the start of the EDCOR program, which provided a chance for a peaceful life versus a hunted life.[74]

The Philippine government knew in 1951 that it could not h repeat the scandalous and violent 1949 elections. In a public statement, Magsaysay vowed that the elections would be honest and peaceful. He stuck to his word. In order to ensure the increased legitimacy of the election process, he increased military presence, deploying active duty, reserve and ROTC cadets to ensure the security of polling places and cast ballots. He also enlisted the assistance of JUSMAG officers to ensure further the legitimacy of the elections. Despite the Huks' concerted effort to disrupt the elections, there were minimal deaths. The surprising outcome of the elections was that Quirino's Liberal Party lost control of the Senate to the Nacionalista Party. Despite the success of the COIN campaign, many felt that Quirino had only implemented government reforms to stop the Huks, and not help the populace. The elections also showed the increased popularity of Magsaysay, because his interest lay in helping the people through governmental reforms.[75]

Magsaysay's increasing popularity and commitment to the people compelled him to run for the presidency as a Nacionalista Party member. In his resignation letter to President Quirino, he wrote that he could continue to hunt and kill Huks, but the problem remains the same: corruption, neglect, poverty, and land reform. In November 1953, Magsaysay won the election with the largest margin in Philippine history. After assuming office, he implemented the long

---

[73] Ibid., 129.
[74] Ibid., 130.
[75] Ibid., 133.

desired land reforms and other economic reforms, while maintaining the EDCOR program. In an ironic twist, many peasants joined the Huks, and immediately surrendered, just to participate in the EDCOR program.[76]

With the initiative firmly in the hands of the government, the military launched the largest anti-Huk operation of the campaign. OPERATION LIGHTNING-THUNDER consisted of 5,000 troops and lasted 211 days. At the conclusion of the operation, the AFP had captured 88 Huks, killed 43 and accepted the surrender of 44 while sustaining minimal casualties. The most significant outcome of the operation was the surrender of Luis Taruc and his Chief of Staff. Concurrent with this operation, the Second Military District conducted operations with similar success. The combat operations of 1954, combined with Magsaysay's civic programs and reforms, effectively ended the Huk insurgency in the Philippines.

The Manwaring paradigm principles were evident in phase two of the COIN operations. Magsaysay integrated the six paradigm principles to defeat the Huks, and restore order to the islands. Through his campaign design, he integrated a military offensive and civic approach to end the insurgency. Magsaysay enlisted financial and advisory support from the U.S to defeat the Huks. The financial aid package allowed him to pay salaries, which were in arrears, and to develop the capabilities needed to defeat the Huks. The financial aid package also allowed him to implement civic action programs as a measure to restore the government's legitimacy and moral authority. Magsaysay clearly understood that the AFP's terror tactics had to end. The security situation in the Philippines would further erode if discipline in the AFP was not restored. The military's discipline also translated to reducing external support to the insurgents. Popular support for the Huks decreased as relations between the populace and the military improved. This principle, in conjunction with intelligence source operations, isolated the Huks from the populace, and limited their operational reach.

---

[76] Ibid., 138.

THE FARC IN COLUMBIA

Background

The case study of the Revolutionary Armed Forces of Colombian (FACR) differs significantly from the Philippine case study. First, the duration of the Colombian insurgency has already exceeded the Philippine insurgency. The Philippine insurgency lasted only five years, while the Colombian insurgency has existed since 1966. Secondly, although both insurgencies were Marxist-Leninist based, the FARC arguably focused on drug trafficking profits. Lastly, analysis of the Colombian insurgency reveals underlying issues associated with the Manwaring paradigm. At issue are the principles of legitimacy and military and other support to the affected government.

In addition to the issues concerning the Manwaring paradigm, the Colombia case study also revealed political factors not fully appreciated by the Manwaring paradigm. The political considerations in determining success criteria often affect the tactical and operational level of war.

Revolution in Colombia

The roots of the FARC insurgency date back Colombia's La Violencia, a national political process. La Violencia describes the political process in Columbia during the period from 1946 to 1964; the level of violence was highest from 1948 to 1953. La Violencia was the result of two related causes that set the stage for Fidelista and Guevarist revolutionary warfare. First, the elites of opposing parties sought to impose a national model for modernization. Second, local partisanship affected people from all races, class groups and large regions. In addition to these two factors, the Cold War fueled the liberal-conservative division throughout the social strata.[77]

---

[77] Safford, 345.

The political measures to end La Violencia further divided the conservative and liberal parties and oppressed the population. President Laureano Gomez Castro lost popular support because of his oppressive measures, attacks on moderate Conservatives and the military. Gomez fell ill in 1951 and allowed his first president designate Roberto Urdaneto Arbelaez to become acting president. Although Urdaneto followed Gomez's policies, he refused to dismiss General Gustavo Rojas Pinilla. Pinilla was suspected of conspiring to overthrow the government, which later proved true. Pinilla, supported by moderate Conservatives, deposed the Gomez government. His first priority was to implement measures designed to end the Violencia, but his government eventually reversed course and pursued a policy of repression.[78] The policy of repression lasted over the next fourteen years and set the stage for a revolution in Colombia.

Fidel Castro regime saw the upheaval as the perfect opportunity to export revolution to the masses in Colombia. It was during this period of La Violencia that insurgencies rose in Colombia. Colombian Fidelistas returning from Cuba created the guerilla Army of National Liberation (ELN) in 1965. The following year, the pro-Moscow Colombian Communist Party (CPP) created the Revolutionary Armed Forces of Colombia (FARC). The next revolutionary group to enter the struggle was the Maoist group People's Liberations Army (EPL) in 1967. The final revolutionary group to form was M-19.[79]

The numerous insurgent organizations competed for popular support and resources. The FARC grew to become the largest and most capable organization despite this competition. The FARC leader, Manuel Maralunda Velez, widely known as Tirofijo (Sureshot), started his guerilla career during the early stages of La Violencia. He was a member of a liberal guerilla organization in Tolima, which was an epicenter of the political violence. In 1964, Maralunda

---

[78] Hanratty, 33-40.
[79] Anthony James Joes, Guerilla Warfare: A Historical, Biographical, and Bibliographical Sourcebook, (Westport: Greenwood Press, 1996), 146.

helped establish a communist-oriented independent republic in Marquetalia.[80] The independent

republic ended because of a May 1964 military attack on Tolima. According to the guerillas, a

16,000-man force sponsored by the U.S. government attacked 1,000 villagers. The survivors

formed the FARC because they believed that armed conflict was the only way to achieve their

political ends.[81]

The FARC's first priority was to ensure its survival. It had to gain control of territory and

arm and equip its forces. The FARC's actions are indicative of past insurgent actions. An

insurgency is most vulnerable during the strategic defensive, and operations are limited to gaining

support, defense, territorial control and gaining resources. Their operations through the early

1980s were, therefore, limited in scope and intensity. In its early stages, the FARC focused its

military efforts on small farm raids and ambushes against military forces. The objective of the

offensive operations was to gain weapons, military equipment, food and other supplies. The

FARC also targeted and attacked those viewed as government informants. The FARC lacked the

operational and tactical reach to venture out of areas under their direct control. They did not

achieve the operational capability to expand their guerilla front until 1969.

The FARC commenced its second guerrilla front in 1969 with the aim of expanding its

influence into the Magdalena Valley. The guerillas later opened fronts in Uraba and Santander.

The 1971 front in Uraba was strategically important because the FARC gained control of the

Darien gap between Panama and Colombia. Their control of the Darien Gap isolated the

Colombian government from Panama, and gave the FARC border access to a second country. In

furtherance of their manifesto, the FARC established a general staff and a secretariat to provide

political direction for their struggle.[82]

---

[80] Angel Rabasa and Peter Chalk, Colombian Labyrinth: The Synergy of Drugs and Insurgency and Its Implications for Regional Stability (Santa Monica: RAND, 2001, MR-1339), 24.
[81] Center for International Policy, "Colombia Project". Site at http://www.ciponline.org/colombia/index.htm, accessed on 24 January 2004
[82] Rabasa, 24.

The latter half of the twentieth century was marked by engagements between the military and the various guerilla groups. The weakness of the various guerilla numerous groups was their inability to unite and overthrow the government, despite similar leftist ideologies. Even in the face of success in countries such as Nicaragua and Cuba, where separate organization formed alliances; the groups in Colombia could not even form tactical alliances. The FARC distinguished itself from the other organizations by its ability to gain materiel and financial support. The FARC turned to kidnappings, and extortion to finance its requirements. Later in the 1980s they turned to drug trafficking as a means of financial support[83]

The FARC expanded in the 1980s by gaining popular support and exploiting the drug trade. President Belisario Betancur initiated cease-fire negotiations with the FARC to head off their growth. The La Uribe accords permitted the FARC to form a legal political party called the *Union Patriotica* (UP). The UP contained disarmed guerillas, Gaitanists and former communists. The UP advocated anti-corruption, anti-drugs, and progressive land and economic reforms.[84] President Betancur believed that the insurgency was over, but he was wrong. The Colombian government failed to understand the objectives and end-state of the FARC. The Manwaring paradigm did not address this aspect of COIN. Marxist-Leninist insurgencies do not seek equal representation within the government. They desire a communist based government. The FARC's participation in the Columbian government was a means to its political end. The FARC negotiated from a position of strength, and it was, therefore, illogical to believe that the insurgency would end through negotiations. During the cease-fire, the FARC quietly expanded its influence and control over the eastern plains cattle market, the oil industry in Magdelana Valley and the gold industry in Antioquia.[85]

---

[83] Ibid., 146.
[84] Online News Hour. "Colombia's Civil War: Revolutionary Armed Forces of Colombia (FARC). Site at http://cocaine.org/colombia/farc.html, accessed on 23 January 2004.
[85] Rabas, 25.

The UP was very successful in winning national and municipal elections and party expansion. The party's popularity and belief in land and economic reform made it a target of right wing and paramilitary organizations. The two organizations began a systematic murder campaign against prominent UP leaders and committed over 3,000 murders. The assassination of a leading UP presidential candidate ended the period of relative peace. The FARC believed that their aims, once again, could not be achieved through the political process, and armed conflict renewed.[86]

The FARC continued its expansion after the failure of the Uribe accords. Their territorial expansion led into the coca producing areas of Colombia. The FARC viewed the drug trade as one of the major social problems in Colombia. The FARC wanted to expand, but did not have the financial resources to do so. Drug trafficking was the solution to the problem. During the seventh conference in 1982, the FARC developed a policy of taxing the drug trade in the areas and routes they controlled and recruited personnel from the lower end of the drug industry. The conclusions of the seventh conference also coincided with the movement of drug traffickers and their paramilitary forces into these cocoa producing regions and the economic dominance of drugs. The FARC realized that it could lose social support because of its involvement in drug trafficking. The agricultural migrants would pledge their support to the Colombian government if the FARC did not consider their needs. The FARC therefore assumed the responsibility of promoting and protecting the coca fields.

The FARC profited economically and militarily from the drug trade. In the 1990s, they added nine additional fronts and moved closer to Colombia's economic and population centers. From their initial 1966 strength of 350 guerillas, the force grew to 15,000 to 20,000 fighters with over 70 fronts by 2000.[87] According to 1998 Colombian government figures, the FARC and

[86] Online News Hour. "Colombia's Civil War: Revolutionary Armed Forces of Colombia (FARC). Site at http://cocaine.org/colombia/farc.html, accessed on 23 January 2004.
[87] Rabbas, 26.

various other organizations annually receive $551 million a year from the drug trade, while receiving only $311 million from extortion and $236 million from kidnappings. These analysts also believe, without empirical evidence, the drug trade is in furtherance of the FARC's grand strategy.[88]

In a March 1999 interview with *El Tiempo*, Marulanda stated that advances in growth and capabilities brought the FARC to a new stage, which forced the Colombian government into negotiations. They would continue their struggle until the final victory. Colombian analysts believe the FARC has three strategic objectives. The first objective is to consolidate control over coca regions in the south and the east. The consolidation will allow the FARC to build-up their forces and expand into other regions of Colombia. The second objective was their expansion of operations throughout the entire country. This objective would force the Colombian government to disperse its forces throughout the entire country, thereby reducing its ability to maintain the initiative. The third objective was the isolation of Bogotá and other major cities. Bogotá relies upon a few easily interdicted roads for overland communications with other countries. The final objective is a large scale offensive to overthrow the government.[89] Marulanda's statements and the Colombian government's analysis led to the conclusion that the FARC was prepared to conduct a strategic offensive against the government. The FARC's ability to transition to a strategic offensive in the 1990s created a crisis in the Colombian government.

The central point of the crisis was the government's inability to exercise control and authority within its territorial borders. In other words, its sovereignty was in question. There are four components to a sovereign nation: exercise complete political control authority over its national sovereignty, monopolizes the instruments of the legitimate use of force, controls its borders and conducts foreign policy with other nations, which recognize its authority. The Colombian government only controls the last two components of sovereignty. The Colombian

---

[88] Ibid., 32.

government's failure is not in its perceived legitimacy, but in its inability to exercise the four components of sovereignty, which Manwaring paradigm's does not address. National sovereignty has four components: "a sovereign state" should exercise complete political control and authority over its national sovereignty, monopolizes the instruments of the legitimate use of force, controls its borders and conduct foreign policy with other nations which recognize its authority."[90] The government has failed to exercise complete control and authority over its national sovereignty. The FARC's controls the southern region of Colombia (estimated at 40%)[91]. The government also failed to monopolize the instruments of the legitimate force. The government is competing for the right to control the southern region with the FARC, the ELN, paramilitary units and drug cartels. There are currently five competitors vying for internal political control. The FARC, UAC, ELN, criminal gangs and the drug cartels are all fighting to exercise control and authority, which only serves to compound the problem and decrease the likelihood of a peaceful settlement.[92] The Manwaring paradigm describes a government's legitimacy as crucial to success in COIN operations. The Colombian government is suffering from a lack of control and law enforcement, not legitimacy. The government effectively controls 60% of the territory, with the FARC enjoying approximately 5% popular support from the populace. Manwaring's proposition on legitimacy does not account for components of sovereignty, which should be included in the paradigm.

Another aspect of the government's problem is the military's inability to secure these affected regions. In mid-2002, Colombia only had 60,000 to 80,000 soldiers to fight against the

---

[89] Rabassa and Chalk, 39-45.

[90] Marcella Gabriel, The United States and Colombia: The Journey from Ambiguity to Strategic Clarity, (Carlisle Barracks: Strategic Studies Institute, U.S. Army War College, 2003), 7, Richard L. Millet, Colombia's Conflicts: The Spillover Effects of a Wider War, (Carlisle Barracks: Strategic Studies Institute, U.S. War College, 2003), 4.

[91] Marcella Gabriel, The United States and Colombia: The Journey from Ambiguity to Strategic Clarity, 16.

[92] Marcella Gabriel, The United States and Colombia: The Journey from Ambiguity to Strategic Clarity, (Carlisle Barracks: Strategic Studies Institute, U.S. Army War College, 2003), 8, Richard L. Millet,

three guerilla organizations and the drug cartel. Along with defeating the FARC, the military must also protect the electrical, gas, road and communications infrastructures from attack, and effectively patrol over 18,000 kilometers of roads and waterways. The military's size is a function of the government's historical political ideology. Colombian elites have traditionally preferred a weak central government and weak military to ensure their place in the social strata. This resulted in a military force that was under-resourced, undermanned and too dispersed to secure the country.[93] Colombia's military weakness and lack of capability is the result of design and financial commitment. The fear of military coups prevented an expansion and required funding to ensure an adequate presence throughout the country and defeat internal threats. The military's primary problem is that its adversary shares near parity in terms of funding and capability[94].

Insufficient funding was evident during President Ernesto Samper's administration when internal violence increased. Instead of increasing military funding, the government reduced it. This created a condition in which the military lacked the adequate resources to accomplish its mission. Colombia is divided into five military regions commanded by the armed forces. Each regional commander is under the authority of the Minister of National Defense. The Colombian government did not organize a national campaign to defeat the insurgents. Each of these five regional commanders, with their assigned forces is conducting their own COIN campaigns against the FARC and other insurgent organizations. In addition to the lack of unity of effort at the national level, the armed forces failed to consider the benefits of joint operations. Plan Colombia was the answer to developing an organized national effort to defeat the FARC.[95]

Colombia's Conflicts: The Spillover Effects of a Wider War, (Carlisle Barracks: Strategic Studies Institute, U.S. War College, 2003), 4.
[93] Ibid., 10.
[94] Marcella, 12.
[95] Marcella, 20.

Plan Colombia

In conjunction with the U.S. government, President Andreas Pastrana formulated Plan Colombia. The plan has ten elements, which address economic, government and judicial reforms, peace negotiations, strengthening the military, counter-narcotics operations and social assistance and reforms. The plan purpose is to break the links, which perpetuate the cycle of violence and discord within Colombia. Profits from the drug trade sustain and increase the capability of the FARC and other organizations, which results in the continuing presence of paramilitary forces. Diminishing or eliminating the drug trade would eliminate the guerilla's resources, thereby preventing them from conducting attacks. This in turn would invalidate the reason for the existence of paramilitary defense forces. These results would further provide the impetus for the guerillas to negotiate a peace settlement, because they would have little reason to wage war against the government and themselves. The FARC insurgency represents a departure from past insurgencies in that outside aid for the insurgents does not come from the populace[96]. The FARC does not enjoy a high level of populace support (2% to 4% populace support). The FARC uses force to recruit members into its organizations. It also uses terrorism directed against the populace to ensure its unhindered drug industry and societal compliance. The FARC's involvement with the drug trade has taken them away from their ideological message and aim. This prevents them from effectively using propaganda as a means to question the government's authority.[97] The FARC's primary financial support comes from drug trafficking. The United States' interest is primarily the interdiction and reduction of drug trafficking.[98]

U.S. policy states that the security of Colombia is of vital interest to the United States. The U.S. policy toward Colombia supports the U.S. concern for controlling the illegal cultivation and exportation of cocaine and heroin. The pervasiveness of the drug trade was not only harmful

---

[96] Marcella, 20.
[97] Marcella, 20.
[98] Marcella, 20.

to the social structure of Colombia, but had a tremendous negative impact in communities throughout the U.S. The Drug Enforcement Agency (DEA) estimated that Colombia produces over 80% of the world's cocaine supply and three percent of the world's heroin supply. The U.S. consumes over seventy percent of the drugs produced in Colombia. These two facts alone make the security and stability of the Colombian government a vital U.S. interest. The links between drug trafficking and guerilla activities and paramilitaries are well known. Through the drug trade profits, these organizations have developed the capability to control numerous regions throughout Colombia. This control of the rural areas further increases the marginalization of the population within the controlled regions. For these reasons, the Reagan and Clinton Administrations pledged support to counter drug trafficking in Colombia and foster peace.[99]

The counter-drug theory is supported by mutually reinforcing initiatives, which incorporate other initiatives by drug consuming countries such as the U.S. Critical to the plan's success is the establishment of a secure environment to support the other elements of the plan. In addition to an undermanned and over-tasked military, the Colombian military is struggling to conduct joint and unified operations. The Colombian Army controls the country's five military districts. These district commanders have historically conducted COIN operations independently, which is the reason the effort is disjointed. The guerillas, having near military parity, have either successfully defended their territory or moved into other military districts to prevent defeat.[100]

The near military parity between the FRAC and government forces affects Colombia's "Southern Strategy"; a direct attack against the FARC's center of gravity. The strategy supplements the ongoing efforts to interdict drugs and chemical precursors, to eradicate coca and poppy field and destroy coca labs. Seizing control of the Putamayo region, a major coca-

---

[99] Congress, Senate, Committee on Foreign Relations, *U.S. Policy Toward Colombia: Hearing before the Committee on Foreign Relations*, 106th Cong., 3rd session., 6 October 1999.
[100] Gabriel Marcella and others, *Plan Colombia: Some Differing Perspectives*, (Carlisle Barracks: Strategic Studies Institute, U.S. Army War College, 2001), 3, Hanratty, 281.

producing region, is the first phase of the strategy. The second phase of the campaign is an expansion of the counter-narcotics operation to encompass the entire country.[101]

U.S. Support to Plan Colombia

The U.S government is the primary provider of military support to Colombia. In conjunction with U.S. security interests in Colombia, the U.S. pledged support to fight international drug trafficking. The original plan envisioned a total contribution of $5.7 billion, of which the U.S. pledged $1.3 billion over a five-year period. Colombia pledged $4 billion ($3.5 billion in U.S. foreign assistance) with Europe providing the rest. The U.S. allocation of funds encompassed all elements of Plan Colombia, but came with conditions.

Manwaring's paradigm defines military support to the targeted government in terms of military funding, materiel, training and other resources. The paradigm does not address the nature of the supporting government's policies and objectives. The U.S. government has placed conditions on the military support to Colombia. These conditions include investigation and possible prosecution for alleged human rights abuses by the military and paramilitary, development of a JAG corps and development of a strategy to eliminate all poppy and coca production by 2005. The human rights concern is a byproduct of the 1997 Leahy Amendment. This amendment "prohibits military assistance to foreign militaries that violate human rights with impunity". This creates a question of practicality given the nature of COIN operations. History has shown that human rights violations occur within the context of such operations. Even the well-trained and disciplined U.S. military was guilty of human rights violations in Vietnam.[102]

The human rights violations in Colombia, however, were appalling. From 1993-98, the Colombian Commission of Jurist and human rights groups indicated that security forces, paramilitary groups and the guerillas were involved in political killings, disappearances and

---

[101] Rabasa, 64.
[102] Rabasa, 63.

social cleansings. It is important to note that over this five-year period, killings by the military

had declined, while guerilla and paramilitary killings increased annually. This shows that there is

a correlation between the increasing drug trade and measures taken to ensure production and the

paramilitary's response.[103]

The military assistance program to Colombia helps them execute their "Southern

Strategy" by training and equipping its new counter-narcotic battalions. In addition, this

assistance provides programs designed to improve the Colombian Navy's ability to control traffic

along the country's 18,000 km navigable waterways. U.S. aid will also support improvements in

radar, airfields and intelligence collection capabilities. The strategy to eliminate drugs is the

primary support for military operations without considering the adaptability of the FARC and

other insurgent organizations in Colombia.

A turning point in U.S. support to Colombia's counter-narcotic campaign occurred after

the 911 terrorist attacks. The Bush Administration's recognition of Colombia's complex and

deeply ingrained security problems marks a major change in U.S. assistance to Colombia. This

problem is a function of the Colombian government's inability to exercise its authority within the

confines of its border. The inability to control the five regions has allowed guerillas and drug

traffickers to violate the sovereign borders of its neighbors. The government's weakness created

an environment in which, illegal activities occur with impunity and only adds to the societal

degradation of those regions. These factors foster the conditions, which breed terrorism.[104]

The COIN operation to eliminate the FARC and other insurgent organizations is ongoing

and no end is in sight. The FARC's decision to use drug trafficking as a source of financial

support marked a key turning point in the insurgency and methods of external support to the

Colombian government. The government's critical failure in the campaign is its inability to

---

[103] Ibid., 63, Gabriel Marcella and Donald Schulz, *Colombia's Three Wars: U.S. Strategy at the Crossroads*, (Carlisle Barracks: Strategic Studies Institute, U.S. Army War College 1999), 9.
[104] Marcella, 1.

exercise control and authority within its borders. The strategy to eradicate drug trafficking as a means to ending the insurgency is faulty, because the FARC is an adaptive organization. This case study shows that the insurgent and terrorist organizations are adaptive organization, which will alter its methods to ensure survival.

The Colombian government is slowly taking the necessary measures to defeat the FARC insurgency. The flaw in their actions is the campaign to eradicate drug trafficking. To this end, the United States has pledged continuing support in the counter-drug effort. The U.S. support to Plan Colombia shows the implications of support to a targeted government. The United States' interest in eradicating drugs has clouded the efforts to defeat the insurgency. It also does not support the strategic aim in the war on terrorism. Insurgent warfare is a form of political violence to achieve a political end. The FARC will adapt to the eradication of coca, and develop other financial means. One such method is to sponsor terrorist sanctuaries and training bases in Colombia. The U.S. government has focused solely on one component of the FARC system.

The Colombian case study reinforces the need to understand insurgencies and terrorism before applying Manwaring's principles to the war on terrorism. This case study represents a departure from a holistic approach to COIN operations. Plan Colombia focuses on one aspect of the FARC insurgency without considering the nature of insurgencies. Military planners must link Manwaring's principles to operational and tactical action. The belief that drugs are the center of gravity has formed the core of U.S. support to Colombia. The Colombian Army's military capability and training is, therefore, linked to counter drug forces and not counter-guerilla operations

CONCLUSIONS AND RECOMMENDATIONS

Defining success in the war on terrorism begins with understanding the operational environment. The terrorist mentality and motivation is tone aspect of defining success. Physical effort and cognitive capabilities are key instruments to this success. Western mental models do not provide the cognitive basis to determine success criteria. The western mind looks for logic as the basis for action and motivation. The moral code of democratic societies fails to understand that morality is relative to culture and belief systems. While terrorist acts seem despicable and cowardly, they achieve the political end state for terrorists. The rush to brand terrorist acts as barbaric only serves an information campaign to stir a nation's emotions. It does not help to solve the problem if the government and the military fail to understand the sources of motivations.

Religious and political ideology also motivates the terrorist action. The ideology is linked to perceptions of relative deprivation. It is important to note that deprivation needs only to be perceived and may not be real. These beliefs are eggshell thin, but are nearly impenetrable. Negotiations will not work and appeasement is futile. The ideology is too ingrained and pervasive to believe that a peaceful settlement is possible. The ideology drives action with near impunity. Terrorists that are motivated to become suicide bombers do not fear international legal systems. Transnational terrorist organizations have taken advantage of this fact. The adversary does not have a readily identifiable structure or doctrine for operations.

Dr. Manwaring provides the framework for defining success in the war on terrorism. He derived the six principles with a full understanding of the operational environment. Case study analysis was the method to highlight the development of the principles and the operational and tactical requirements to achieve the strategic aim. The Philippine and Colombian case studies served this purpose. Both case studies showed the adaptive nature of an insurgency. The Huks were able to survive the early phase of the insurgency because they understood the terrain and the capabilities of the Philippine constabulary. Like the Huks, the FARC established its base of operation in restricted terrain.

The Philippine government survived the insurgency because Ramon Magsaysay led the counter-insurgency. Magsaysay had a distinct advantage. He was a guerilla fighter during World War II. He understood insurgents and knew how to defeat them. Through his actions, he exemplified Manwaring's principles. Magsaysay's COIN campaign was a holistic approach to not only defeating the Huks, but also ensuring long-term sustainment. Magsaysay's success also points to issues not addressed in the Manwaring principles. Long-term commitment is vital to a society free from insurgency. Manwaring died before fully implementing his civic programs and economic and social reforms. The succeeding administration did not understand the imperative of long-term sustainment. The conditions for future insurgencies were set because the next administration failed to understand this imperative.

The Colombian study analysis offered a different view of the Manwaring paradigm. The Colombian government does not have a Ramon Magsaysay to fight the FARC. The principles of legitimacy and military and other support to the targeted government are at issue. The Colombian government does not exercise authority and control over 40% of its territory. The FARC has no base of popular support, yet the insurgency still exists. The Colombia government's legitimacy is not in question. Its ability to regain control of the affected areas is the crux of their problem. The U.S. pledged support to Colombia, but the support focuses on drug eradication. Manwaring states that military and other support to a targeted government is crucial to defeating an insurgency. The U.S. government has pledged its support to drug eradication but not direct efforts to defeat the FARC. The Leahy Amendment placed restrictions on U.S. military training support to foreign militaries. The U.S. trained the Colombian military to conduct counter-drug operations and not counter-guerilla operations. Magsaysay clearly understood the need to train the Philippine Army to defeat the Huks. In this instance, political constraints and restraints have influenced operational requirements. The implications will manifest itself in future operations in the war on terror. Despite the differences between the case studies, they are fundamentally the same.

The insurgencies formed from an ideology. A small vanguard of individuals perceived the current situation as untenable and unacceptable. The dissatisfaction with the current social economic and social conditions produced the discontent. Silence or inaction is not the means to achieve a change in the current state. Insurgents and terrorist politicize discontent to garner support and sympathy from the masses. The unifying theme promises a way of life that is more equitable for all. Both the FARC and the Huks politicized their discontent and formed a base of support to produce change. The unifying message for change was communism. At the point when political violence served as a means to an end, both insurgent organizations focused on controlling terrain, survival, low level attacks and propaganda. The ways and means employed by the FARC and the Huks are similar to all insurgencies. An enduring facet of the two insurgencies, and all insurgencies for that matter, is adaptation.

The FARC and the Huks (until March 1950) displayed the traits of complex adaptive systems. Insurgencies are composed of numerous agents or functions that interact with each other in numerous ways to achieve a common goal. The small organizations within the system, such as the Barrio United Defense Corps, self organized to resist Japanese control and provide intelligence. Despite the lack of insurgent doctrine, these organizations developed elaborate systems of intelligence operations, materiel procurement, propaganda and tactics. Historically, insurgents mastered the terrain and exploited the advantages it provided. Both the FARC and the Huks controlled the restrictive terrain of their respective countries. The Colombian and Philippine militaries proved powerless in their efforts to dislodge the insurgents. Attempts by both military forces were ineffective, because the effort focused on one component of the system. Colombians and the Philippines directly attacked the insurgents without understanding the interaction of the components within the system. The guerillas are but one component of the complex system. Magsaysay unknowingly viewed the Huks as a system and developed a strategy to unhinge systems components. The Colombian government's Plan Colombia is a systems approach to end the decades' long insurgency. Only time will tell if this approach will end the insurgency.

In the end, the Manwaring paradigm is a useful tool to define success in the war on terror. The end-state in the war on terrorism is the reduction of the operational reach and capability of terrorist organizations. Reducing a terrorist organization's operational reach and capability will confine these organizations within a controllable region. This will reduce terrorism to criminal acts, thereby moving terrorism to a law enforcement issue. The ideology cannot be defeated, and, therefore, efforts at public suasion are not proper measures of success in the war on terrorism. The terrorist mentality and motivation provides the conceptual framework to develop a comprehensive campaign plan, which considers the intangible aspects of the threat. Manwaring's paradigm provides successful principles to measure success. Understanding the operational environment links the Manwaring paradigm to the end-state. A thorough review and update of joint and service doctrine will provide the framework to facilitate planning for success. The combination of Manwaring's paradigm, knowledge of the operational environment and doctrine review and revision will lead to success.

The war on terror and the associated national strategy for combating terrorism provides the strategic guidance for future military operations. The nature of war has changed. Now more than ever, war is deeply rooted in the human dimension. The adversary does not have a physical system to attack. The U.S. military has no peer competitor in conventional warfare. The adversary understands the U.S. military capabilities. Therefore, the adversary will employ unconventional tactics to gain a level of near parity. Terrorist organizations will use insurgent tactics, techniques and procedures to level the battlefield. In this regard, the institutional military must fulfill the requirements of the operational military.

One method of preparing the force is to instill a systems thinking approach to develop the cognitive capabilities necessary in operational art. Even though the analysis supports Manwaring's principles, the criteria are force oriented. With the exception of legitimacy and organization, the principles imply reliance on offensive operations. Defining success in the war on terrorism is more than the sum of battles and engagements. The U.S. military must defeat terrorist organizations, but it must also reduce the underlying conditions that breed terrorism. The Philippine case study showed a holistic approach to defeat the Huks. Terrorist organizations are complex adaptive learning systems. The mechanical approach of applying firepower to the problem is not always affective. Firepower is the U.S. military's forte, but the end-state in the war on terrorism focuses on reduction, not destruction or annihilation. Introducing systems thinking in military education will imbue the planner with a powerful cognitive tool to support planning and execution.

In support of systems thinking, effects based operations needs to come to a resolution. The complex environment in the war on terrorism merits debate on the utility of effects based operations as a tool in operational art. A government's action against an insurgent system produces effects to a determined order. Effects based operations, in theory, suggest that secondary and tertiary effects are measurable. It is time to put the theory into joint doctrine. By doing so, it will end the theoretical propositions and bind it within the confines of reality. Effects based operations support the systems approach to operational design because it forces planners to consider secondary and tertiary effects beyond the immediate desired effect.

BIBLIOGRAPHY

Asprey, Robert B. *War in the Shadows: The Guerilla in History.* 2 vols. Garden City: Doubleday and Company, Inc., 1975.

_____. *War in the Shadows: The Guerilla in History.* 2nd ed. New York: William Morrow and Company, Inc., 1994.

Barrens, Clarence G. "I Promise: Magsaysay's Unique PSYOP 'Defeats' Huks." Masters Thesis. U.S. Army Command and General Staff College, 1970.

Batschelet, Allen W. Effects Based Operations: A New Operational Model? Carlisle Barracks, Pa.: USAWC Strategy Research Project, U.S. Army War College, 2002.

Becker, Michael, D. *Operational Art in Counterinsurgency Campaign Planning.* Newport: Department of Operations, Naval War College, 17 June 1994. DTIC, ADA 283523.

Beckett, Ian F.W. *Encyclopedia of Guerilla Warfare.* New York: Checkmark Books, 2001.

_____. "Forward to the Past: Insurgency in Our Midst," *Harvard International Review* 23, no. 2 (Summer 2001): 59-63.

_____. *Modern Insurgencies and Counter-insurgencies: Guerillas and their Opponents since 1750.* London: Routledge, 2001.

_____, ed. *The Roots of Counter-Insurgency: Armies and Guerilla Warfare, 1900-1945.* London: Blanford Press, 1988.

Benson, Kevin C.M. and Christopher B. Thrash. "Declaring Victory: Planning Exit Strategies for Peace Operations". *Parameters.* Autumn 96, pp. 69-80.

Birtle, Andrew, J. *U.S. Army Counterinsurgency and Contingency Operations Doctrine 1860-1941.* Washington, DC: Center of Military History, 1998.

Blaufarb, Douglas S. *The Counterinsurgency Era: U.S. Doctrine and Performance.* New York: The Free Press, 1977.

Bracamonte, José A.M. and David E. Spencer. *Strategy and Tactics of the Salvadoran FMLN Guerillas: Last Battle of the Cold War, Blueprint for Future Conflicts.* Wesport: Praeger, 1995.

Bunge, Frederica M. *Philippines: A Country Study.* Washington, DC: U.S. Government Printings Office, DA PAM 550-72, 1984.

Cable, Larry E. *Conflict of Myths: The Development of American Counterinsurgency Doctrine and the Vietnam War.* New York: New York University Press, 1986.

_____. "Reinventing the Round Wheel: Insurgency, Counter-Insurgency, and Peacekeeping Post Cold War," *Small Wars and Insurgencies* 4, no. 2 (Autumn 1993): 228-262.

Callwell, Charles E. *Small Wars: Their Principles and Practice,* 3d ed. London: His Majesty's Stationary Office, 19XX. Reprint, Lincoln: University of Nebraska Press, 1996.

Campbell, Arthur. *Guerillas: A History and Analysis.* New York: The John Day Company, 1968.

Central Intelligence Agency. "Philippines" in *The World Factbook 2002.* 1 January 2002. Site at http://www.cia.gov/cia/publications/factbook/geos/es.html. Accessed on 10 September 2003

Chalk, Peter. "Re-Thinking U.S Counter-Terrorism Efforts". Washington D.C.: RAND Corporation, 2001. Database on-line. Available from http://www.rand.org/hot/op-eds/092101SDUT.html

Chapman, William. *Inside the Philippine Revolution.* New York: W.W. Norton & Company, 1987.

Childress, Michael. *The Effectiveness of U.S. Training Efforts in Internal Defense and Development: The Cases of El Salvador and Honduras.* Santa Monica: Rand, 1995.

Clausewitz, Carl von. *On War.* Edited and translated by Michael Howard and Peter Paret. Princeton: Princeton University Press, 1976.

Clutterbuck, Richard. *Guerrillas and Terrorists.* Ohio University Press, Chicago: 1980

Comish, Leo S., Jr. "The United States and the Philippine Hukbalahap Insurgency: 1946-1954." USAWC Research Paper, US Army War College, 1971.

_____. "Military Doctrine and the 'Learning Institution:' Case Studies in Low-Intensity Conflict." Ph.D. diss., University of Southern California, 1995.

Davis, Paul K, and Brian Michael Jenkins. "The Influence Component of Counterterrorism: A Systems Approach," *RAND Review.* Spring 2003.

de Wijk, Rob. "The Limits of Military Power," *The Washington Quarterly* 25: 1 (Winter 2002): 75-92.

Dillon, Dana R. "Comparative Counter-insurgency Strategies in the Phillipines," *Small Wars and Insurgencies* 6, no. 3 (Winter 1995): 281-303.

Dorner, Dietrich. *The Logic of Failure.* New York: Metropolitan Books, 1989.

Downes, Richard. *Landpower and Ambiguous Warfare: The Challenges of Colombia in the 21st Century.* Carlisle Barracks: Strategic Studies Institute, U.S. Army War College, 10 March 1999.

Downie, Richard D. *Learning From Conflict: The U.S. Military in Vietnam, El Salvador, and the Drug War.* Westport: Praeger, 1998.

Fall, Bernard B. *Last Reflections on a War.* Garden City, New York: Doubleday & Company, Inc., 1975.

Flavin, William, "Planning for Conflict Termination and Post-Conflict Success". *Parameters.* Autumn 2003, pp.95-112.

Flynn, Stephen E. U.S. Support of Plan Colombia: Rethinking the Ends and Means. Carlisle Pa. U.S. Army War College. Strategic Studies Institute, May 2001.

Gottlieb, Aryea, "Beyond the Range of Military Options." *Joint Force Quarterly.* Autumn 95, pp. 99-104.

Gray, Collin S. "Thinking Asymmetrically in Times of Terror". *Parameters.* Spring 02, pp. 5-14

Greer, James K. "Operational Art for the Objective Force," *Military Review* 82, no. 5 (October 2002): 22-29.

Golay, Frank, H. *The Philippines: Public Policy and National Economic Development.* Ithaca: Cornell University Press, 1961, 71-72. Quoted in Dana R. Dillon, "Comparative Counter-insurgency Strategies in the Phillipines," *Small Wars and Insurgencies* 6, no. 3, 285, (Winter 1995).

Grant, Thomas A. "Government, Politics, and Low-Intensity Conflict." In *Low-Intensity Conflict: Old Threats in a New World.* ed. Edwin G. Corr and Stephan Sloan, 257-275. Westview Studies in Regional Security, ed. Wm. J. Olson. Boulder: Westview Press, 1992.

_____. "Little Wars, Big Problems: The United States and Counterinsurgency in the Postwar World." Ph.D. diss., University of California, Irving, 1990.

Gray, Colin S. *Defining and Achieving Decisive Victory.* Carlisle, Pa.: U.S. Army War College. Strategic Studies Institute, 2002.

Greenberg, Lawrence M. *The Hukbalahap Insurrection: A Case Study of a Successful Anti-Insurgency Operation in the Philippines, 1946-1955.* Washington, DC: Analysis Branch US Army Center of Military History, CMH Pub 93-8, 1986.

Griffith, Samuel B. *Sun Tzu: The Art of War.* New York: Oxford University Press, 1963.

Guevara, Ernesto "Che". *Guerilla Warfare.* New York: Monthly Review Press, 1961. Reprint, Lincoln: University of Nebraska Press, 1985.

Gurr, Ted Robert. *Why Men Rebel.* Princeton: Princeton University Press, 1970.

Hammer, Kenneth. "Huks in the Philippines," *Military Review* 36, no. 1, (April 1956): 50-54.

Holland, John. *Hidden Order: How Adaptation Builds Complexity.* Reading: Helix Books, 1995.

Institute for International Mediation and Conflict Resolution. "The World Conflict and Human Rights Map 2001." Site at http://www.iimcr.org/imgs/Conflictmap %202001-g.pdf.

International Monetary Fund Staff. "Globalization: Threat or Opportunity?" April 12, 2000 (Corrected January 2002). Site at http://www.imf.org/external/np/exr/ ib/2000/ 041200.htm. Accessed on 10 October 2003.

Jenkins, Brian Michael. "Terrorism: Current and Long Term Threats", Santa Monica: *RAND* Corporation, November 2001. Database on-line. Available from http://www.rand.org/publications/CT/CT187/

Joes, Anthony James. *America and Guerilla Warfare.* Lexington: University of Kentucky Press, 2000.

Johnson, Stuart Martin, ed., "New Challenges, New Tools for Defense Decisionmaking", Washington D.C.: *RAND* Corporation, 2003. Database on-line. Available from *http://www.rand.org/publications/MR/MR1576/MR1576.pref.pdf*

Joint Forces Staff College. *The Joint Staff Officer's Guide 2000.* 2000.

Joint Publication 1-02: *Department of Defense Dictionary of Military and Associated Terms.* Washington, DC. 2001

Joint Publication 3-0. *Doctrine for Joint Operations.* 10 September 2001.

Joint Publication 3-07. *Joint Doctrine for Military Operations Other than War.* 16 June 1995.

Joint Publication 3-07.1. *Joint Tactics, Techniques, and Procedures (JTTP) for Foreign Internal Defense(FID).* 26 June 1996.

Joint Publication 5-0. *Doctrine for Planning Joint Operations.* 13 April 1995.

Joint Publication 5-0. *Doctrine for Joint Planning Operations(2nd Draft).* 10 December 2002.

Joint Publication 5-00.1. *Joint Doctrine for Campaign Planning.* 25 January 2002.

Kerkvliet, Benedict J. *The Huk Rebellion: A Study of Peasant Revolt in the Philippines.* Berkeley: University of California Press, 1977. Reprint, Lanham: Rowman & Littlefield Publishers, Inc, 2002.

Kitson, Frank. *Low Intensity Operations: Subversion, Insurgency, Peace-keeping.* Harrisburg: Stackpole Books, 1971.

Klien, Gary. *Sources of Power.* Cambridge MA: The MIT Press, 1998.

Lachica, Eduardo. *The Huks: Philippine Agrarian Society in Revolt.* New York: Praeger Publishers, 1971.

Lansdale, Edward G. *In the Midst of Wars: An American's Mission to Southeast Asia.* New York: Harper & Row, Publishers, 1972. Reprint, New York: Fordham University Press, 1991.

Laurie, M.I. "The Operational Level in Low Intensity Conflict," *Low Intensity Conflict and Law Enforcement* 1, no. 3 (Winter 1992): 312-323.

Leech, Garry M. *Killing Peace: Colombia's Conflict and the Failure of U.S. Intervention.* New York: Information Network of the Americas, 16 August 2002.

LeoGrande, William M. *Our Own Backyard: The United States in Central America, 1977-1992.* Chapel Hill: The University of North Carolina Press, 1998.

Luvaas, Jay. "Lessons and Lessons Learned: A Historical Perspective." In *The Lessons of Recent Wars in the Third World, Volume I*, ed. Robert E. Harkavy and Stephanie G. Neuman, 51-72. Lexington: Lexington Books, 1985.

Manchester, William. *American Caesar: Douglas MacArthur 1880-1964.* Boston: Little, Brown and Company, 1978.

Mann, Edward C., III, Gary Endersby, and Thomas R. Searle. *Thinking Effects: Effects-Based Methodology for Joint Operations*, CADRE Paper No. 15. Maxwell Air Force Base: Air University Press, 2002.

Manwaring, Max G. *Internal Wars: Rethinking Problem and Response.* Carlisle Barracks: Strategic Studies Institute, U.S. Army War College, September 2001.

_____. *Nonstate Actors in Colombia: Threat and Response.* Carlisle Barracks: Strategic Studies Institute, U.S. Army War College, May 2002.

_____. "Toward an Understanding of Insurgency Wars: The Paradigm." In *Uncomfortable Wars: Toward a New Paradigm of Low Intensity Conflict,* ed. Max G. Manwaring, 19-28. Westview Studies in Regional Security, ed. Wm. J. Olson. Boulder: Westview Press, 1991.

_____. *U.S. Security Policy in the Western Hemisphere: Why Colombia, Why Now, and What is to Be Done?.* Carlisle Barracks: Strategic Studies Institute, U.S. Army War College, June 2001.

Marcella, Gabriel. *Plan Colombia: The Strategic and Operational Imperatives.* Carlisle Pa. U.S. Army War College. Strategic Studies Institute, April 2001.

_____. The United States and Colombia: The Journey from Ambiguity to Strategic Clarity. Carlisle Pa. U.S. Army War College. Strategic Studies Institute, May 2003.

Marcella, Gabriel and Donald Schulz. *Colombia's Three Wars: U.S. Strategy at the Crossroads.* Carlisle Barracks: Strategic Studies Institute, U.S. Army War College, 5 March 1999.

Mendel, William W. and Floyd T. Banks. "Campaign Planning: Getting it Straight," *Parameters* 18, no. 3, (September 1988): 43-53.

Metz, Steven. *Counterinsurgency: Strategy and the Phoenix of American Capability.* Carlisle Barracks: Strategic Studies Institute, U.S. Army War College, 28 February 1995.

_____. "A Flame Kept Burning: Counterinsurgency Support After the Cold War," *Parameters* 25, no. 3, (Autumn 1995): 31-41.

_____. "Counterinsurgent Campaign Planning," *Parameters* 19, no. 3, (September 1989): 60-68.

_____. *The Future of Insurgency.* Carlisle Barracks: Strategic Studies Institute, U.S. Army War College, 10 December 1993.

Millet, Richard L. *Colombia's Conflicts: The Spillover Effects of a Wider War.* Carlisle Barracks: Strategic Studies Institute, U.S. Army War College, October 2002.

Mintzberg, Henry. *The Rise and Fall of Strategic Planning: Reconceiving Roles for Planning, Plans, Planners.* New York: The Free Press, 1994.

Morrissey, Michael T. *End State: Relevant in Stability Operations?* Fort Leavenworth, KS: U.S. Army Command and General Staff College, May 2002.

O'Neill, Bard E. *Insurgency & Terrorism: Inside Modern Revolutionary Warfare.* Dulles: Brassey's (US), Inc., 1990.

Paget, Julian. *Counter-Insurgency Operations: Techniques of Guerrilla Warfare.* New York: Walker and Company, 1967.

Passage, David. *The United States and Colombia.* Carlisle Barracks: Strategic Studies Institute, U.S. Army War College, March 2000.

Peterson, A.H., G.C. Reinhard and E.E. Conger, eds. *Symposium on the Role of Airpower in Counterinsurgency and Unconventional Warfare: The Philippine Huk Campaign.* Santa Monica: RAND, RM-3652-PR, July 1963.

Rabasa, Angel and Peter Chalk. *Colombian Labyrinth: The Synergy of Drugs and Insurgency and Its Implications for Regional Stability.* Santa Monica: RAND, 2001.

Romulo, Carlos P. and Marvin D. Gray. *The Magsaysay Story.* New York: The John Day Company, 1956.

Rose, Donald G. "FM 3-0 *Operations*: The Effect of Humanitarian Operations on US Army Doctrine," *Small Wars and Insurgencies* 13, no. 1 (Spring 2002): 57-82.

Rosello, Victor "Lessons From El Salvador," *Parameters* 23, no. 4 (Winter 1993-94), 100-108.

Roskin, Michael G. "Crime and Politics in Colombia: Considerations for U.S. Involvement,". *Parameters.* Winter 01-02, pp. 126-134.

Sanger, Richard H. *Insurgent Era: New Patterns of Political, Economic, and Social Revolution.* Washington, DC: Potomac Books, Inc., 1967.

Schirmer, Daniel B.and Stephen R. Shalom, eds. *The Philippines Reader: A History of Colonialism, Neocolonialism, Dictatorship and Resistance.* Boston: South End Press, 1987.

Schwarz, Benjamin C. *American Counterinsurgency Doctrine and El Salvador: The Frustrations of Reform and the Illusions of Nation Building.* Santa Monica: RAND, R-4042-USDP, 1991.

_____. Guerilla Warfare: A Historical, Biographical and Bibliographical Sourcebook. Westport: Greenwood Press, 1996.

Schulz, Donald E. "The Growing Threat to Democracy in Latin America," *Parameters*, Spring 01, pp. 59-71

Shy, John and Thomas W. Collier. "Revolutionary Warfare." In *Makers of Modern Strategy: From Machiavelli to the Nuclear Age*, ed. Peter Paret, 815-862. Princeton: Princeton University Press, 1986.

Slade, Stuart. "Successful Counter-insurgency: How Thais Burnt the Books and Beat the Guerillas," in *Internal Security & CO-IN,* an editorial supplement to *International Defense Review 22,* (October 1989): 21-25.

Strange, Joe. *Centers of Gravity & Critical Vulnerabilities: Building on the Clausewitizian Foundation So That We Can All Speak the Same Language.* Quantico: Marine Corps University Foundation, 1996.

Summers, Harry G. Jr. "A War Is a War Is a War Is a War." In *Low-Intensity Conflict: The Pattern of Warfare in the Modern World,* ed. Loren B. Thompson, 27-49. Lexington: Lexington Books, 1989.

Taruc, Luis. *He Who Rides the Tiger: The Story of an Asian Guerilla Leader.* New York: Frederick A. Praeger, Publishers, 1967.

Thompson, Leroy. *The Counterinsurgency Manual.* London: Greenhill Books, 2002.

Thompson, Robert. *Defeating Communist Insurgency: Experiences from Malaya and Vietnam.* Studies in International Security: 10. London: MacMillan Press, Ltd., 1966.

Toase, Francis. "The French Experience." In *The Roots of Counter-Insurgency: Armies and Guerilla Warfare, 1900-1945*, ed. Ian F.W. Beckett, 40-59. London: Blanford Press, 1988.

Trinquier, Roger. *Modern Warfare: A French View of Counterinsurgency.* With an introduction by Bernard Fall. Translated by Daniel Lee. New York: Frederick A. Praeger, 1964.

Turabian, Kate L. *A Manual for Writers of Term Papers, Theses, and Dissertations.* 6th ed. Chicago: University of Chicago Press, 1996.

U.S. Census Bureau. "World Population Profile: 1998 – Highlights." Site at http://www.census.gov/ipc/www/wp98001.html.

U.S. Congress. Senate. Committee on Foreign Relations. *U.S. Policy Toward Colombia: Hearing before the Committee on Foreign Relations.* 106th Cong., 3rd sess., 09 October 1999.

U.S. Department of Defense. *National Strategy for Combating Terrorism.* Washington, D.C., 2003.

U.S. National Security Council Staff. "A Report to the President by the National Security Council with Respect to the Philippines." NSC 84/2. 9 November 1950. In *The Philippines Reader: A History of Colonialism, Neocolonialism, Dictatorship and Resistance*, ed. Daniel B. Schirmer and Stephen R. Shalom, 105-110. Boston: South End Press, 1987.

U.S. President. Address. "Address to a Joint Session of Congress and the American People." Office of the Press Secretary (20 September 2001): site at http://www.whitehouse.gov/news/releases/2001/09/20010920-8.html, accessed on 25 January 2004.

U.S. President. Remarks "Remarks by the President to the United Nations General Assembly." Office of the Press Secretary (10 November 2001): site at .

Valeriano, Napoleon D. and Charles T.R. Bohannan. *Counter-Guerilla Operations: The Philippine Experience.* New York: Frederick A. Praeger, Publisher, 1962.

Waldrop, Mitchell M. *Complexity.* New York: Simon and Schuster, 1992.

Williams, Thomas J., "Strategic Leader Readiness and Competencies for Asymmetric Warfare". *Parameters.* Summer 03, pp. 19-35.